Unlock Your Brain Code

In loving memory of Dr. Courtland Ofelt

Unlock Your Brain Code:

Why You Haven't Manifested What You Want and How to Fix It

Kat Tsoncheva

First Printing: 2015

Editor: Casey Greenberg

ISBN 978-0-692-49409-7

Ekaterina Tsoncheva
Las Vegas, NV

Contents

Introduction 1

Part 1: Attitude 9
   Wanted and Unwanted 9
   What Defines Your Attitude 13
   The Power of Your Habits of Thought 18
   Did You Charge Your Brain? 24
   Inner Conflict Drains Your Power 26
   Reptile Brain 28
   Brain's Rescue Mission 31
   Enemies or Friends? 35
   The Strength of Your Desire 42
   Wanted or Unwanted? Where Your Attitude Is 45
   In the (Manifesting) Zone 50
   The Shower Phenomenon 56

Part 2: Clearing the Mind Immobilizers 59
   Somebody Needs to Be in Charge 59
   Worry 64
   Guilt 75
   Not Knowing Your Worth 93
   Blame 106
   The Need to Control What You Can't 111
   Fear of Failure 123
   Is Your Comfort Zone Getting Uncomfortable? 127
   Release the Attachment to the Outcome 131
   Processes to Help You with Mind Immobilizers 134

Part 3: Changing Beliefs 146
   Challenging the Boundaries 146
   The Guards of Your Belief System 151
   Changing Beliefs 156
   Harnessing Your Attention 158
   Belief is Contagious 163
   Changing Patterns 167

Part 4: Quick Start Guide 177

The Blueprint 177

Acknowledgements 185

References 186

Introduction

Have you ever wondered about the force that so generously gives love, abundance and success to some, while it leaves others struggling? What is it that makes dreams come true for those lucky few? Is it some special advantage that they were born with or good luck?

When we look at successful people in any area of life, we often look at the end result and assume that they are people who were born with either an extraordinary brilliance or good luck. It seems like they were somehow chosen. Success simply happened to them. You imagine that Steve Jobs took a bite out of an apple and Apple computers materialized. Thomas Edison saw a flash of light when he hit his head stumbling around in his basement and invented the light bulb. Alexander Bell conjured a telephone of out scrap wire, simply because he missed a long distance friend.

Well I'm here to say that no, success did not simply happen to them. Steve Jobs dropped out of College; Thomas Edison was removed from school for being "slow." Alexander Bell had to harness sound waves long before he could even consider the phone. These were not men born with a "Success Guaranteed" stamp on their birth certificate. They also suffered hardship and setbacks. But they achieved success in the end. So you can too: Rest assured that you still have the same power those men had that can make the journey to your dreams a successful one. This book will teach you how to unleash that power and make it work for you, rather than against you. It is not anything extraordinary or special. It is something that you were born with. And while none of us were given user manuals at birth, you can still learn how to operate this amazing potential.

In the pages to come, you will take a journey from the inception of a desire, all the way through its growth and the mind conditions that allow it to unfold and come to full manifestation. You will read about astounding results from various studies as well as experiments that will show you that not everything we've learned is what it seems to be. The science of human behavior suggests that there are better and much more efficient ways to achieve the perfect mindset for realizing a desire. This book will teach you how to achieve your goals, but more importantly, it will give you enough knowledge to troubleshoot the areas that don't work and fix them easily. It will teach you how to harness the power of the universal laws, so they can finally work for you.

You will be able to transform your life into the life that you would like to have. You have all that it takes. Your mind has a potential much bigger than you may have realized. You could have anything that you desire: from better health, to a financially abundant life. You could have harmonious relationships, joyful experiences, peak performances, high achievements or anything else that you would like to manifest: The principles of success work for everybody.

It is not a matter of whether the principles of success will work for you; it is a matter of you understanding how they work, so that you can successfully use your mind to create the life that you desire.

You have unlimited potential in your mind, like a dormant genius, just waiting for you to awaken it. Knowing your potential is the first step, but remember, just knowing that you have the potential won't wake the genius up. You need to understand how to tap into the potential, how to successfully use the potential. And, if you think that your life is so busy that you don't have time to invest in sharpening your tool, think again: you have the exact same amount of time that life gave to Thomas Edison, Alexander Bell and Steve Jobs.

Let me use a metaphor here. Imagine that you are running a business and you are looking for a powerful software program that can help you with your needs. When you search for software, you make your purchase selection based on the product description. The product description highlights all the great things the program can do for you. You read, you like, so you buy. You are excited about all the enhancements you are about to get from the program.

Well, hearing the fact that you can create anything you want in your life by harnessing the power of your mind is you only reading the product description: "Dear customer, if you buy into this idea, you will be able to reach your goals, fulfill your desires and manifest a happy, healthy and fulfilling life." Then, when you read success stories of people who have overcome illness by nothing more than their focused mind, or people who built powerful business empires from ground zero, or people who realized a beautiful relationship, these stories are part of the testimonial section in the product description. These are the satisfied customers who bought into the idea, used it and now are living the success promised in the product description.

Let's get back to that software program. You've bought it, installed it on your computer, and you're eager to start seeing the results! But when you open the program, you see a screen full of buttons, scroll bars, panels and menus. Oh, boy! You look at the product description, showing easy results. Then you look at the complicated, busy screen in front of you and realize that in order for you to get all the wonderful promises in the product description, you have to first learn how to use the software. If you start using it without understanding how it operates, you could click on a button and your whole right panel would disappear. You try to do simple tasks but it would seem like the program had a mind of its own. Sometimes it worked, sometimes it didn't. It's like how your printer works perfectly one day, but then, it decides it doesn't want to print anymore the next day and you have no idea why. The same is with the principles behind realizing your desires. You've read the product description and you've already determined "I want this NOW!" You may even have the list of pending desires, sorted in the order of urgency, ready for your magic wand to start materializing. But if you want to be a master of your magic wand and to successfully create what you want, you need to familiarize yourself with how the magic wand works. More importantly, when it doesn't work, knowing how to troubleshoot and fix the problem. And I promise you, it's a lot easier than it sounds.

So let's start breaking down those buttons.

Life is a series of cause-and-effects and if-then statements. The reason why we feel discouraged and overwhelmed is the confusion coming from the lack of predictability and understanding. You don't understand exactly how your present choices are affecting your future outcome. Think about it, if you could predict with relative accuracy which choices would affect you positively or negatively ahead of time, how many great things would you do in your life?

I was recently having dinner with a friend. Half a year ago, he was excited about expanding his practice by using the power of his mind. He was reading about different visualizations, meditations and manifesting processes. He was studiously applying the processes, but half a year later, results were still not forthcoming. He was disappointed and so, he pronounced that mental power doesn't work. He pointed out the fact that millions of people read self-help books, but only a very small percentage of them become successful, therefore the odds were against him. He said that there are so many processes out there, but there is no universal step-by-step process that would serve success up on a platter. And while he's wrong about the Universal laws not working, he is right about success not being a one size fits all. If we all had minds that were exactly the same, meaning the same belief systems, the same past experiences that defined us, the same attitudes, and the same childhoods, then there could be a universal process that could work for everybody. But we all have very unique and highly complex minds and what works for one, may not work for somebody else. Each individual mind is a different software program. Because of that, there is no cookie-cutter solution. It has to be customized for each specific person by that person. That's why using someone else's methods without understanding how they work could be good for some, but it could also be spinning wheels with no results for others.

In this instance, my friend bought into the idea that he could create a better life for himself. He had read the happy customers reviews in different self-help books and materials and got inspired. However, what he hadn't done was first learn how to use his mental software program. Because of that, my friend couldn't control the process. The program seemed to have a mind of its own. And just like when a computer program starts acting weird on you, you want to unplug the damn thing and start all over. In this moment of disappointment, of frustration, he proclaimed that manifesting his desires was something that simply does not work.

But let's start with the basics. First off, you are the creator of your own mindset. It is your mindset that determines what manifests in your life, as well as in your actions. Your mind is like a powerful filtering engine that can filter in and out anything you want or don't want. You may want to have a bank account with seven figures, but if your mindset is pointing in the opposite direction, then there is no way for it to manifest in your life.

Imagine shopping for a sweater in an online mega store. When you start browsing, you use filters to narrow down your search. You don't need to look at every item sold in the store, so you select the clothes category to filter out everything else. Then, you filter out the colors that you don't like and narrow down your search to a small selection of what you are looking for. Your mind functions much in the same way in creating your reality. Only this time it's not the click of the mouse that narrows what manifests on your screen, but your mindset on the subject. You may want more money, or your soul mate, or a new fancy car. It doesn't matter what your religion is, it doesn't matter if you deserve it, it doesn't matter if you've been good, it doesn't matter what your current circumstances are, it doesn't matter what anybody else says about it. Your wish is immediately ready to start unfolding without any judgments or restrictions. Once your mental settings are pointing in the right direction, your desires are ready to be fulfilled.

The creation of your desires is made up of three main components. They are the three components that form your mindset on a specific subject and determine the speed at which the manifestation will be realized. These three components are:

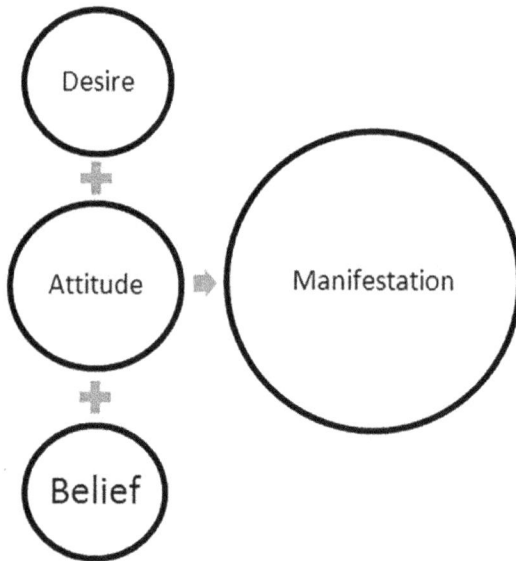

```
   (Desire)
      +
  (Attitude) ➡ (Manifestation)
      +
   (Belief)
```

Each of these components has its own part in the book where you will be guided to understanding of what each component entails, and how to remove the blocks standing in your way to achieve success in each component. This is because creating your desire is not a matter of whether you will be granted your wish by a higher power or not. It is only a matter of removing the mental blocks that have been preventing you from having it. The moment you come up with a desire, it is ready to start unfolding.

Part 1: Attitude

Wanted and Unwanted

Death Valley is one of my favorite places to visit. Most of the time, there is nothing but mud hills, rocks, and perfect silence. Life is scarce there and it could stay that way for years. Then there are those special years when something magical happens. In Springtime, the normally barren lands are transformed into a spectacular display of wildflowers that make the ground look like a yellow carpet. The little seeds spend years in the ground, waiting for the perfect combination of well-spaced rainfall, sufficient warmth from the sun, and lack of the usual desert winds. When the conditions are right, a beautiful transformation happens in the valley that attracts people from all over the world.

In the same way the conditions necessary for the wildflowers to transform Death Valley into a spectacular display of colors must be just right, your desires also need the right conditions in your mind to start realizing success in your life. Remember how we said that any manifestation has three main components - desire, attitude and belief? Well, Beneficial Conditions are having these three components all aligned in the same direction.

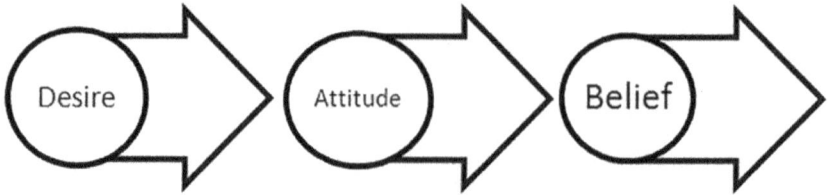

Desire → Attitude → Belief

The right attitude is the most important and often the hardest part of the equation. If the attitude is set toward the desired outcome, you already have much better chances of switching your beliefs.

Let me explain.

When you have a desire, you have two realities. One is the current reality. The other one is the possible future reality. It's like solving a problem: the problem is the current, unwanted reality, while the solution is the possible future, wanted reality. The desire starts with recognizing the unwanted reality. Without a problem, you have no desire for a solution. For example, if the problem is you don't have enough money, it creates a desire for enough money. If you already have enough money, then there is no reason to stir desire. When you initially recognize the problem, the unwanted reality, your inner balance becomes temporarily disturbed. This is the motivation that starts focusing your resources into the realization of your new desire. If your attitude is pointing to the solution, soon enough, things start changing.

Before we can jump into talking about bigger desires, let's start with a simple one. Because this part of the book explores the "Attitude" component, we will look at a wish that has the "Desire" and the "Belief" components already aligned: a desire to have a more organized closet. This is a desire that you believe you can have - there is nothing miraculous or unbelievable about having an organized closet.

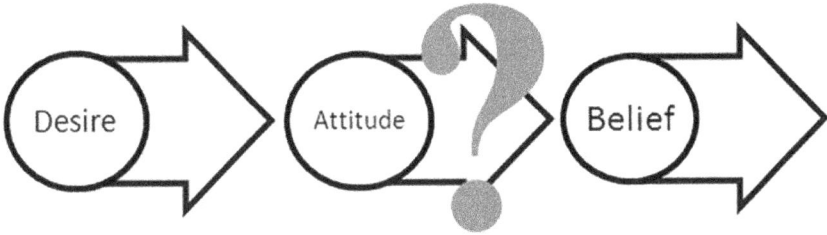

In this case, the problem is the clutter, and the solution is the better-organized closet. The moment you recognize that you don't want the clutter anymore, you've come up a desire for an organized closet. The unwanted situation creates the initial motivation for a change. Your attitude will determine the success or the failure of your desired result. If you have an attitude of complaining about the clutter or feeling powerless against the clutter, the clutter continues to govern your closet and not much is done.

So your attitude can either support the current reality that focuses on your clutter, or the future desired reality. You always have these two opposite points of each subject - the unwanted and the wanted. If your attitude is pointed more toward the unwanted reality, the unwanted reality stays active. If your attitude switches to focus on the desired reality, it gradually takes precedence until that reality becomes the active one. It's like your mind activates or inactivates each of the opposite points of a subject, depending on your attitude and focus.

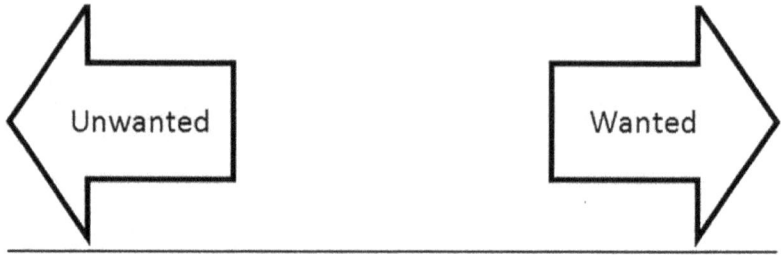

Subject

Attitude can point to each of the two sides of the subject and activate it.

What Defines Your Attitude

Let's take a few moments to define what "attitude" is. According to the Webster dictionary, it is "a mental position with regard to a fact or state; a feeling or emotion toward a fact or state."

What happens when you think "closet?" Where exactly is the idea of the "closet" concept located in your brain? You can search left and right but you won't find it. Unlike your home, it doesn't have a specific place in the brain layout. There is no "closet" section. It is not because the "closet" idea is too small to notice. It is quite the opposite. When you think of "closet," a complex map of neural connections is activated, all based on your prior experience and knowledge. These neural connections are not firing in only one section. The data about your closet is spread in a large, complex network area that forms your entire idea of closets. Not only that: Your idea of closets is different from my idea of closets. Everybody has a unique and different perception of the same subject.

When you think "closet," this may activate childhood memories. It may awaken the pain and suffering you endured when you had to sacrifice precious Playtime for the completely unnecessary chore of cleaning your closet. It may activate other concepts, such as managing your house or managing your life. It may painfully remind you that there is a huge list of things that need to be managed if you only had a cloned version of yourself to help. It may connect to memories of perfect closets you've seen in magazines (do they really exist?). It may activate feelings of guilt for having allowed your closet to become such mess. It may also link you directly to the couch - a safe escape in the face of a closet cleaning threat. The idea "closet" is constantly being updated and reinforced by your life experiences, which in turn molds your attitude on the subject and could predominantly point toward what you want or toward what you don't want. This is valid for any concept that you hold you in your brain. These complex network connections form your personality and your future experiences. In a way, your inner being emerges through the networks in your brain. We could call them Habits of Thought.

These associations are not just pure data of prior experience either. They each have a smaller or bigger emotional tag attached to them. Your brain is wired to ensure your survival, which it does by classifying experiences as beneficial for your survival and experiences as dangerous for your survival. In a way, it categorizes the world around you into "friends" and "enemies." For example, if you touched the hot stove when you were a kid, touching a hot stove was classified as a dangerous experience, therefore an enemy. Your pillow, on the other hand, is a friend. It never fails to give you the perfect comfort to send you into a nourishing sleep, proving the pillow beneficial for your survival. Or maybe you originally viewed something as a friend and then it became an enemy. A box of prunes can be delightful, until you eat the whole box. Then suddenly your supposed friend becomes an enemy when you spend the rest of the day being tortured in the bathroom. As far as your brain is concerned, the world is represented by threats and rewards.

Back to the closet: If you associate your closet with a feeling that you are failing to manage your increasing demands in life, thinking about the closet will give you the emotional warning that the subject is your enemy. You may feel anxious, nervous, overwhelmed or sometimes depressed. Even though there is a desire for a clean closet, the underlying habitual pathways keep the attitude pointed toward the unwanted reality. You may think, "Clutter is hard to overcome" or "My life has become unmanageable." If, on the other hand, you associate the closet with fun and creativity, your brain will give you the 'this is a friend' green light!

So can you deliberately change the direction of your attitude? The answer is yes. You can be a person who is in control of everything, including your closet. As you saw, your attitude is defined by your habits of thought and the emotional tags those habits carry. To change your habits of thought, to start with, you need to be equipped with good Attention Control.

Your attention is what gives power and momentum to your thoughts. The more you put your attention on a thought (or a group of thoughts), the more they come to the foreground of your consciousness. And the opposite is true. If you ignore a thought, it will go in the background, soon to disappear from your awareness. For example, instead of focusing on this page, try focusing on yourself. How is your breathing? You'll notice that by focusing on your breath, you bring to the foreground sensations about your breathing that you may not have noticed before, even though they were there the whole time.

When you focus on a thought, you "activate" it. That thought is at the foreground of your mind. When you remove your attention from a thought, you "inactivate" it and send it to the background.

To make your understanding of "attitude" clearer, let's see what an attitude looks like if it's pointed to what you want as opposed to what it looks like if it's pointed to what you don't want.

Attitude pointed to what you want contains one crucial element: you feel mostly emotionally resolved on the subject. There are no habits of thought carrying the "enemy" tag. When you are emotionally resolved on a subject, there is no (or little) fear, anxiety, blame, or guilt. If you look at your messy closet from an emotionally resolved standpoint, you would see the mess in its true colors: it is nothing more than something that will get done, similar to other items on your to-do list, like noticing that you've run out of shampoo or walking the dog. You don't have to complain about it, you don't have to write in your blog about it, you don't have to talk to your shrink about it; you don't need to go to your friend's house to vent about the situation. When the time is right, the closet transformation begins.

Attitude pointed to what you don't want will incur the exact opposite. You may become anxious or angry. You may feel overwhelmed just by thinking of the closet. You might procrastinate or have to leave the house to take your mind off the subject.

As you can see, your attitude has power that can either realize what you want, or maintain what you don't want. It can either switch to the solution, or stay in the problem. In fact, your attitude has so much power over your reality that if it is strongly pointed to what you don't want, it can blind you to the existence of a solution altogether. You may know clearly what you don't want, but have no clue what you want. Defining what you want out of what you don't want is not always easy.

When I was a teenager, there were a lot of fun things to do. A lot of them were things that my mom would do anything to prevent me from doing. From my perspective, they were fun, adventurous, and exciting. From her perspective, they were dangerous, inappropriate, and potentially bad for my future that she had envisioned. We had a problem: who was going to do the choosing for what I did - was I, or was it my mom going to do it? It put a lot of tension between us that kept growing proportionate to our disagreements. I saw my mom as a very difficult parent. My mom saw the exact same thing: a very difficult daughter. We had built habits of thought around our relationship: that our relationship was difficult. Every time we sat to talk, these habits would play out and our attitudes and expectations were set before we even opened our mouths. During those mom-daughter war times, I knew very clearly what I didn't want. I was unhappy about my mom interfering with my life. At the same time, I had no clue about what I wanted. My way of dealing with the situation was to talk to my friends. We could complain about our moms for hours, giving each other validation that we were right and the "moms" were wrong. This validation would make me even more defensive against mom interference, solidifying my war stands.

One day, my mom came to me and right away I knew that something was different. She had raised the white flag. She said that it's time we defined a solution that would work for both of us. A solution? I had never thought of it. I was so busy knowing what I didn't want that I had no idea what I wanted. In fact, I had no idea that there was even something to want. But that was the day everything started to change. We deliberately decided to step out of our habitual attitudes, and we both put efforts into making the relationship work.

If you are strongly focused on what you don't want, the solution may be right in front of your eyes, but you won't even know it exists because you are not looking for it. You are still defending the problem. To start looking for a solution, you need to define what you want out of what you don't want. It requires stepping out of the habitual thoughts on the subject and tuning into the language of the desire that was born from the unwanted situation. In other words, an unwanted situation will keep torturing you, unless you can define what you want out of it and filter out the habitual thoughts that keep you pointed into the problem.

The Power of Your Habits of Thought

Now let's talk about habits. There is one thing that drives my cat absolutely crazy. It's a freshly opened can of tuna. When the tuna smell reaches her cute little nose, even if she is in the middle of her deepest sleep, she shows up in the kitchen in a matter of seconds, meowing, pacing back and forth, her tail shaking with pleasure and anticipation.

But if I call her name without any tuna promises, she may or may not show up. This is what goes on in her kitty head: "I hear you calling me, but I am really busy right now with more important cat matters like staring at the wall, or taking one of my 20 types of naps, or keeping a keen eye on that fly buzzing around. Like every self-respecting cat, I will show up only when I need your attention."

So I decided to trick her. Every time, before opening a can of tuna, I would tap the tuna can with a spoon. She soon learned that hearing the tap is always followed by the heavenly tuna smell and voila! All I have to do is tap a tuna can and within seconds, I have a little fur ball rubbing at my feet. The tap itself has nothing to do with tuna. I could very well take a can of beans and tap it with the same result. For my kitty, the tap is a sure promise of an immediate reward. Showing up in the kitchen at the sound of the tap is a conditioned response that she has developed, and it works every time. It is an established habit routine, and it is actually nothing more than a case of Pavlov's Dog. Ivan Pavlov was a famous Russian psychologist who studied conditioned responses. Pavlov would ring a bell whenever food was given to the dog. Soon the dog would start associating the ring with food and as a result, Pavlov had a drooling dog whenever the bell rang even when there was no food in sight. [1]

Both in Pavlov's official study, and my own real-life experience, animals and humans are able to develop conditioned responses to stimuli that, over the course of time, begin to happen instinctually. Pavlov demonstrated that these conditioned reflexes can be engrained as deeply and unwittingly as the hard-wired responses you're born with, like your pupils dilating when they see light.

You and I, like everybody else, have built up a system of conditioned responses to different triggers. Think of these responses like shortcuts. A very large percentage of our behavior is a result of automatic responses. This is a very efficient way to deal with our rich stimulus environment. In order to move around and deal with the complexity of our daily lives, we need these shortcuts. Not having to think is translated into efficiency. In fact, every day we accumulate new data through experience and expand the number of automated actions that we can make without thinking. Habits give us that power. Habits make us efficient, automated systems.

When we talk about habits, we are talking about the prefrontal cortex, located behind your forehead, and the basal ganglia, located in the center of your skull. The prefrontal cortex is in charge of decision making, setting up goals, solving problems, self-control, and cognitive functions. It is also the visionary that defines your desires. The prefrontal cortex is the conscious part of the brain that you identify as you. [2] The basal ganglia is in charge of all the habits and learned patterns. When you learned to drive, the whole complex set of body movements of pushing pedals, steering your wheel, and looking in mirrors was processed by your basal ganglia, and converted into an automatic behavior. If it weren't for this brain function, every time you got into your car, you would have to pay conscious attention to each little action, the way you did when you got into a car for the first time in your life. [3]

Imagine how powerful and precise such a system is! The basal ganglia is great at making us more efficient, but it is not that great at looking at the bigger picture. It doesn't understand what a goal is, it doesn't know what you are trying to accomplish, and it would give you a blank look if you said that some of the habits it so readily plays out are bad for your goals. You give it a trigger, and it will immediately execute the habit program - it doesn't matter whether the developed habit is good or bad.

That's where the prefrontal cortex comes in. This brain function is able to see the big picture. It understands, being the portion of your brain that harnesses your desires, that if you are on a diet, it needs to stop the basal ganglia from automatically buying that Sunday night ice cream like it's used to doing every week. But the prefrontal cortex has one major flaw: it gets tired easily. Because its functions are so powerful and because it operates on a broad spectrum, it needs a lot of energy to continue to run. Conscious mental activity uses a lot metabolic resources, which tires both you and your prefrontal cortex out. Maybe you've noticed that your focus is low when you are tired, fighting a cold, hungry or haven't had enough sleep. In those instances, you just didn't have the energy to keep your prefrontal cortex running.

That's why both you and the prefrontal cortex rely on the pre-learned system of habits: it provides efficiency. Once a habit is formed, it can be performed with very little brain effort. The active participation of your conscious prefrontal cortex is not required and so can be diverted to other tasks. Because driving is an automatic habit for you, unless a decision needs to be made that is outside the routine, your conscious attention is not required. You can set your brain on autopilot, and let your learned program take over. In the meantime, you can listen to the radio, talk to the passengers, or let your mind wander to what you want to accomplish next that day.

From your brain's perspective, it would much rather maintain autopilot mode, to relieve the prefrontal cortex of as much effort as possible.

Once a habit is formed, the specific trigger will always initiate the habit program. This is an effortless process. I have a friend, for example, who used to go to Barnes and Nobles to read books. While in the store, one of two things would happen. Either Johnny Cash's "Ring of Fire" would play at some point and she would buy a bag of jellybeans, or it wouldn't play and she would skip the jellybeans and keep reading a book. Without realizing it, "Ring of Fire" had become a trigger for a sweet tooth. Even to this day, almost ten years later, if my friend hears "Ring of Fire" by Johnny Cash, she craves jellybeans. She had formed a habit.

Triggers for your habits could be almost anything, from a specific smell, to a visual trigger, to a mere thought. Habits themselves could be almost anything, from a complex set of steps while driving, to an emotional response, a set of thoughts, or a specific attitude. Habits can even be formed without your conscious awareness of them.

Habits can be so engrained that they even overcome your common sense. If we go back to our closet example, if your habit is to put your attention on the unwanted, every time you think of your closet, you have the "clutter" trigger and the habit plays out: thoughts of how much you hate it and how helpless you feel against it. It's an automatic process that happens when you think about your closet. It's the path of least effort.

Even if your friends get tired of you whining about your clutter and decide to come for a closet-cleaning party at your house where the closet does actually get cleaned, you still haven't changed your habits of thought to being able to have an organized closet. So, a few weeks later, things will start piling up again. Not long after, you will be back to facing your closet situation. You may have had your closet cleaned once, but you didn't establish any habitual thoughts to keep the closet consistently clean for the future. Clean, uncluttered thoughts: clean, uncluttered closet.

You want an organized closet. You can fulfill your organized closet wish. The only thing holding you back is the "enemy"-tagged habits of thought that point to the unwanted reality that is your disorganized closet. Are habits that powerful that you would choose suffering over solution and relief?

The National Institute on Alcohol Abuse and Alcoholism performed a set of experiments to answer this question. Mice were trained to press a lever to get food, until the behavior became a habit (Back to Pavlov's Dog). Then, the researchers poisoned the food to make the mice sick if they ate it. They also electrified the floor, so that the mice walking to their food received a shock. The mice were vomiting and jumping from the electrical shocks: But they still refused to break the habit they had initially been taught to press the lever to achieve food. [4]

Even if we know that a habit is bad for us, it is so ingrained in our brain that we will keep doing it like a zombie, ignoring reason and common sense. And while we are aware of our behavioral bad habits, and we may apply effort to change, we are often unaware that it's our habits of thought that keep our attitude in the unwanted.

But let's not forget who is in charge here! The prefrontal cortex has the authority to override any the habits of thought that you know are bad for you. The prefrontal cortex is the key to unlocking your success and wanted desires. And YOU ARE THE BOSS who holds that key. However, as we talked about, deliberately fighting a habit requires a lot of effort. To change your attitude direction, you have to inhibit the habitual thoughts that don't serve you and direct your attention to the thoughts that are beneficial for your goal. You have to stop the usual flow of thoughts of how unhappy you are with the clutter, and start thinking of realizing an organized closet. Inhibiting and directing thoughts at the same time is a very demanding task. It would be like switching the gas and the brake pedals in your car. To adjust to the new pedals, you have to inhibit the old habit routine while creating a new one at the same time. It requires a lot of concentration from your prefrontal cortex. And while your basal ganglia can keep going until the end of time, without ever breaking a sweat, your prefrontal cortex only has a limited budget of resources.

Let me illustrate.

Did You Charge Your Brain?

As you've learned so far, your prefrontal cortex works from a limited budget of resources. It tires out easily, which it tires you out. Energy management is very important for your brain. So important, that sometimes people expend so much energy, they can't even see something that's right in front of their face.

A very interesting and famous study described by Christopher Chabris and Martin Simons in the book "The Invisible Gorilla" shows some fascinating facts about the limited resource budget of your conscious brain. They created a short film with two teams playing basketball. One team was wearing white shirts, while the other team was wearing black shirts. The viewers were asked to count the number of times the ball was passed by the white team, completely ignoring the black-shirt team. It may not seem like a very difficult thing to do, but the task is very demanding and requires a lot of attention. Toward the middle of the video, a person dressed in a black gorilla suit runs across the court, thumps their chest and then walks away.

If I asked you to watch this video with a similar counting task, do you think you would miss something as obvious and unusual as a person dressed in a gorilla suit? Well, thousands of people have seen the video and half of them didn't notice anything unusual at all. In fact, when they were told about the gorilla, they were sure that it wasn't there - how could anybody have missed something that obvious!

The reason behind this blindness to the obvious is the highly focused attention into the demanding task of counting ball passes among the white-shirt team. The prefrontal cortex is using resources from a limited budget and, when the needs are high, the resources are allocated to those needs only. Everything else is turned off. [5]

While your prefrontal cortex is amazing in its ability to find creative solutions, like wanting to learn to play the piano or strategize your future, it operates from a controlled amount of resources. Because of the high energy that is needed for the prefrontal cortex to operate, there is a limited budget of attention that you can distribute between activities. What happens when the prefrontal cortex becomes tired? It goes on a lunch break and lets your already established habits take over.

But in order to make a shift in your attitude, you have to inhibit your habits of thought, focus your attention, and direct them to the solution, your desired future! So how can your prefrontal cortex handle that?

Before we answer that question, let's look at one more factor: Inner Conflict.

Inner Conflict Drains Your Power

Have you ever felt like the world was weighing on your shoulders, you don't have motivation to do anything, and just about everything seems too hard? If it does, you are experiencing an inner conflict that psychology has coined "Cognitive Dissonance." In short, cognitive dissonance is a state of mental stress and discomfort that you experience when you have one or more contradictory ideas or beliefs at the same time. It can also be experienced if the three components of your desire are not pointing in the same direction.

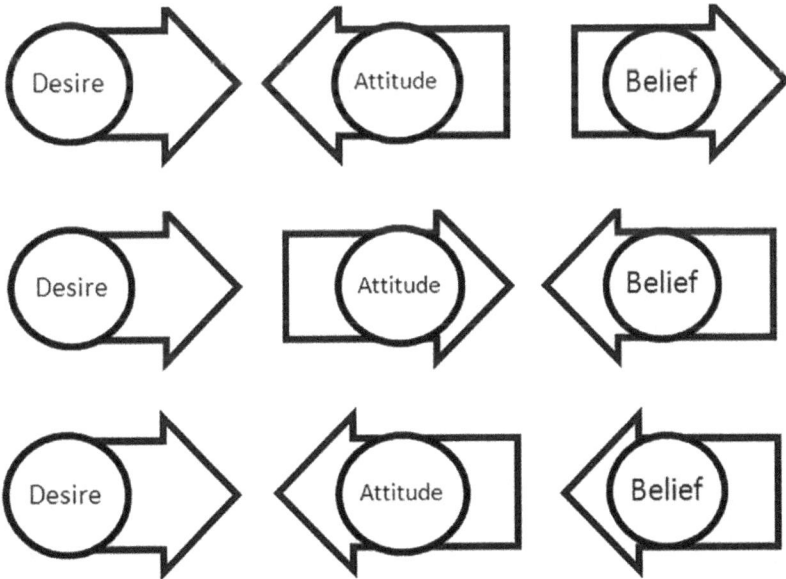

For example, you may want a life of financial ease. Then you look at the pile of bills, your worn out, empty wallet, and you see no way of bridging the two. When a desire is not met by a matching belief or attitude, it results in different degrees of a distressed internal state. It could range anywhere from a mild imbalance, to an extremely stressed condition. Examples of the symptoms of cognitive dissonance are times when you experience worry, guilt, blame, or fear.

If your habits of thought have been pointing to the unwanted, thinking about the closet would create cognitive dissonance. With your closet, you are tired of the clutter, but you feel powerless to make the change.

If you have a subject where your attention habitually goes to the unwanted, every time you think about it, you activate cognitive dissonance, meaning that you are experiencing a smaller or greater amount of stress. Stopping or filtering the habit of thoughts from playing out requires effort: Remember the example with switching the gas and the brake pedal? To be able to handle the effort, you need a strong, present, well-focused prefrontal cortex. Great! But right in the middle of this inner conflict, when you need your prefrontal cortex to take charge, you realize that for some strange reason, your prefrontal cortex has gone for lunch. Stress, in fact, has scared away your prefrontal cortex. Why is that?

Reptile Brain

A long time ago, when humans were living in caves, life revolved around finding something to eat and finding a way not to get eaten. If you lived back then and all of a sudden a wild beast appeared, that would mean immediate danger of being eaten. To ensure that you had what it takes to avoid that danger, nature gave you a very useful mechanism - the "fight-or-flight" response. When there is an approaching danger, your eyes send the signal to the alarm system in your brain, the amygdala. Much like a watchtower that sees the town is about to be attacked, when the amygdala perceives danger, it sounds a warning to the rest of your body. The adrenal gland is activated almost immediately, and it releases the neurotransmitter epinephrine. This triggers the production of cortisol, which subsequently leads to increased blood pressure, blood sugar and the production of glucose. The purpose of this whole set of events is to give you a boost of energy and prepare your muscles for a quick response: you can run as fast as you can or fight for your life. [6] Anything to avoid being eaten!

Your system doesn't want you to start rationalizing and weighing the pros and the cons of each of your movements. You need to act fast and you need to act now! So, to switch your operation to an instinctual level, it inhibits your prefrontal cortex. This is because part of the responsibilities of your prefrontal cortex is self-control and ensuring that you don't act on your impulses. When in danger, your best chances of survival are to actually act on your impulses and instincts! To make it, you have to rely on the speed and precision of already established habits. You may remember times when you were in danger of a collision in traffic and you turned the wheel to avoid it before you consciously realized what was happening. Remember, your routine system is much better at data processing and coordination. Your prefrontal cortex has been asked to take a mandatory break.

Luckily, we don't face the danger of being eaten anymore, but we still tend to activate the "fight-or-flight" response to various degrees quite often. When you are under stress, you perceive some part of your life is endangered, whether it is the safety of your job, your relationships with loved ones, paying the bills on time; whatever it might be. The amygdala, your wonderful personal alarm, stays alert and ready to react at all times. As a loyal worker, it sends the memo to the rest of your body. You may be compelled to flee, which translates in the real world as worry, anxiety, guilt, fear, procrastination —or you may be compelled to fight, which breeds the emotions anger, blame, frustration, irritability, or being overcritical. As a result, your prefrontal cortex functions are decreased. You also tend to perceive the world around you more negatively.

We're not done with the closet yet. We've established the closet is cluttered. We've established that when you look at the closet, you focus on the unwanted, which is the fact that it's cluttered and that the clutter is bigger than you. The brain has dutifully tagged the closet as an enemy. This focus sparks cognitive dissonance, which means you become stressed, anxious, or any other sort of negative emotion that churns up inner conflict. Now we know that this inner conflict tells your amygdala to fire off a warning that danger is afoot in the shape of a closet. The fight-or-flight response sends your prefrontal cortex to lunch, and lets the at-the-ready habits of thought of how powerless you feel against the clutter run undisturbed and unsupervised. Bam! Nothing gets done. Back to where we started. Your inner conflict has successfully pushed your focus right back to the unwanted. We can call this Inner Conflict Cycle.

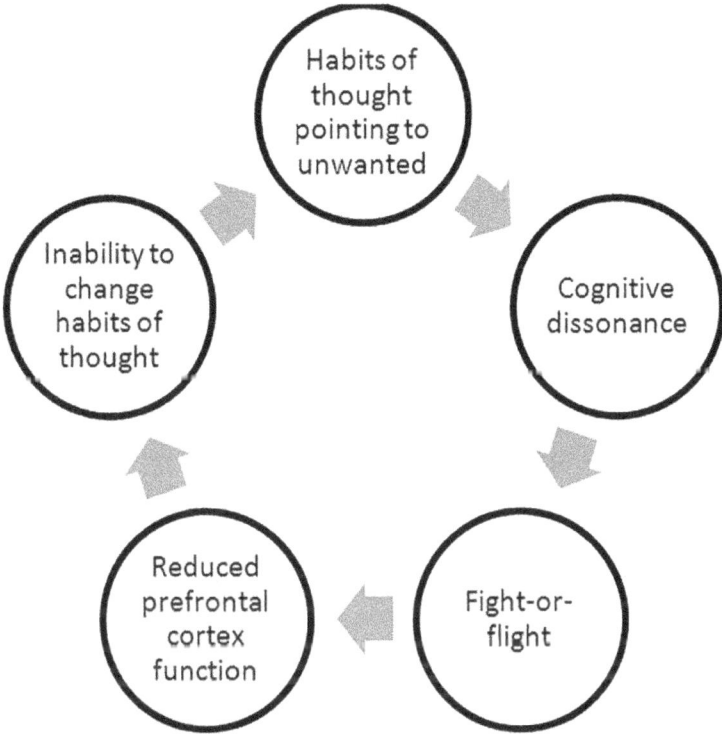

Inner Conflict Cycle

Brain's Rescue Mission

Your brain is amazing in its determination to protect you. You know now that the brain engages the fight-or-flight response to protect you against danger. It is equally determined to protect you against a bad mood. Priority number one is to give you relief. And what would make you feel better but a promise of an immediate reward?

According to the American Psychological Association (APA), the brain copes with the stress by using strategies that activate its reward system: eating, drinking, gambling, smoking, watching TV, surfing the internet, or playing games. The promise of a reward causes release of dopamine - a way for us to find relief and feel better. In other words, your brain finds what it *thinks* will save the day and actively calls your attention there. [7]

How does this relate to cleaning your closet? Well, once the inner conflict cycle gets the better of you, your couch suddenly gains an irresistible, magnetic force. You can't fight the gravity of the immediate reward. The rest on your to-do-list is put on hold, too. You go grab your favorite food and turn your favorite TV show on. For a short moment in time, life is good. No closet monsters to deal with. But a new monster is starting to grow: guilt. Your closet attitude has added the "guilt" nuance, which it will be activated the next time you face the closet.

When you have an inner conflict, not only you are more likely to stay with your habitual behaviors and attitudes, but your brain works hard on to engage you in a reward seeking mission. It wants to make you feel better. We could call this a healing mode. During a healing mode, your resources are used to restore the balance. It is similar to your body entering a healing mode. When you are having a cold, you have specific cravings for things that your prior experience says will make you better. Unconsciously, you are guided to actions and substances that will give you relief. You may all of a sudden start desiring hot herbal tea or chicken bouillon, things that in a normal state do not interest you. Without you being aware of it, your brain is guiding you to what it thinks will give you relief.

Are you beginning to see a cyclical pattern?

Not to worry. Your brain is not your enemy. In fact, you can use this same habit system that is making your failure automatic to make your success automatic. Cognitive dissonance behaviors and habits will be examined and explained with easy steps to solve them. You will learn how to easily create new habits that can harness the same power and use it to your benefit, rather than your disadvantage. You will be able to switch from predominant healing mode to its opposite - growth mode.

When you are in growth mode, the larger part of your resources and mental energies are used to create and reach goals, create and manifest desires, achieve states of higher mental performance and focus and explore your potential. In growth mode, you are not compelled to look for things that soothe you, but for things that excite you. You are happier, with a sense of freedom and forward movement. The state of growth could be occasionally interrupted by periods of healing (when you get angry, upset or react to a situation) but as long as they pass quickly and your predominant mode is growth, you are steadily moving toward your desired outcomes. We all go through times when we lose our balance and react to life, sometimes even several times throughout our day. This is normal. As long as we don't stay there and quickly move back into balance, our predominant mode remains one of growth.

Healing	Growth

Weak Mind

Attention is called to healing
mechanisms

Strong Mind

Attention is called to growth

Whenever there is cognitive dissonance that takes you into the healing mode where your resources are used to restore the inner balance, there's not much is left to promote growth. If your mind is stronger, you enter healing mode less often, and when you encounter an inner conflict, it is resolved quickly, allowing you to return to growth mode. When the mind is weak, inner conflicts stay unresolved and you predominantly stay in healing mode.

Your natural state is one of a strong mind. It is not much different from your body. If you have a healthy body, you have healthy habits. If you have an unhealthy body, this is most likely a cause from having unhealthy habits. I call those negative habits that make you unhealthy Mind Immobilizers, because of their immobilizing effects. We all engage in them. We take them as a natural part of life. In most cases, they are. The problem is when they become chronic and habitual. Such habits are worry, blame, guilt, regret over the past and fear of the future. They are normal: when they are short-lived. In some cases, they could even be positive in the way they can motivate change. The chronic, unresolved habits are the main culprits for a weakened mind. They are habits of thought with "enemy" tags that keep your attention on the unwanted end of the subject and are immobilizing relative to your goals.

Whether you consciously link mind immobilizers to your desires or not, they affect your general idea of how things work. Because they are chronic, they become a familiar part of your experience that you gradually start accepting as normal. When you consider the immobilizers normal, you stop noticing them and you allow them to be a part of your life without second thoughts. Because they keep you in cognitive dissonance over and over, they tire you out and weaken you physically and mentally. Because they activate the fight-or-flight response, not only your cognitive abilities are reduced, you become more defensive on the specific subject and in general (fight-or-flight means danger!).

Mind immobilizers keep you in the inner conflict cycle. As you saw earlier, it is very hard to make a positive change in the middle of an inner conflict. One of two things needs to happen to step out of an inner conflict cycle: make your mind stronger, so that your prefrontal cortex can have the capacity to override the habitual thoughts, or resolve the inner conflict. Clearing the mind immobilizers will give you both. This book will guide you through resolving the most common mind immobilizers: the need to control what you can't, worry, guilt, blame, not knowing your worth, fear of failure, and fear of leaving your comfort zone. As you go through them and start changing your habits of thoughts, you will clear your mental landscape and increase your mental strength. You will also ask your brain to reconsider the "enemy" tags it has placed on different subjects.

Enemies or Friends?

As we mentioned earlier, as part of your survival, your brain categorizes subjects into friends (beneficial for your survival) or enemies (a threat to your survival). Your limbic system is constantly making decisions on what is a friend and what is an enemy. To you, this translates as a weaker or stronger emotional response.

Keeping this in mind, let's take a look at our closet again (since we still haven't cleaned it). In order for a desire for an organized closet to exist, it needs to have the two parts – a messy closet and an organized closet. You can't have a desire for an organized closet if you already have an organized closet. The wanted and the unwanted cannot exist without the other. In fact, the unwanted is the first part of the realization of what you want. If you look at your messy closet and you wish for an organized closet, one way to look at it is to say that the messy closet is the enemy, while the organized closet is a friend. One part is bad, while the other part is good.

And this is where the biggest nugget for your growth is: neither of the two is a friend or an enemy. They are two parts of the whole. If you perceive the messy closet as an enemy, you perceive the whole closet subject as an enemy. If you perceive the messy closet as a friend, the whole closet subject is a friend and change starts happening.

What happens in the brain when you perceive the messy closet as an enemy? You have an inner conflict.

The thing is, for any desire that you hold, until it's manifested, your reality is still representing the unwanted end. This makes it harder to switch your attention away from it. If you define it as an enemy, switching your attention from the unwanted is even harder - your brain is wired to send strong signals when it perceives a threat. The "enemy" response is much stronger than the "friend" response because what's the point of looking for what nourishes you when your existence is in danger. The threat takes priority. My mom always told me that I have to be selective of who I befriend. What I learned much later in life, is how to be selective on what and who I be-enemy.

If, instead of looking at a subject and separate it into its two parts - wanted and unwanted - you see it with real eyes for what it is, you will be able to see that the unwanted is not your enemy. It is an equally good friend as the wanted. I know how absurd this sounds. If you are having hard time paying your bills and about to lose your home, how can you see "not having enough money" as a friend? It is a threat to the existence of what you call home. If you are in pain, how could you call the pain your friend? Yet, the opposite of what you want is what creates the potential for what you want. It activates a subject in your life that gives you room for more growth.

There are not many things that I remember as clearly as my first failure at school. I was thirteen and, until then, I had never had a grade lower than A+. Math was never too hard for me and I was always able to solve the problems without too much thinking. One day, the teacher gave us a harder test. No matter how much I tried, I couldn't solve the problem. I ended up getting an F. I will never forget that day. I cried so much that I couldn't go to school the next day.

What happened that day? In the foreground, it was a school tragedy. In the background, a mild desire that I may have had to be successful in school accelerated into a huge desire. Even though I didn't realize it at the time, the result was there - my desire took a whole new level, ready to unfold. That day, my Mom decided it was time to sit down and help me understand how Math worked. She took a notepad and a pen and our mathematical journey started. Little by little, it started to make sense. But more importantly, I was building a solid knowledge base where I may have left cracks before. Soon, my growing confidence and interest pushed me to look for harder and harder problems. A year later, I was in local and national competitions, one of which won me a scholarship for an elite Mathematical school program. Because of that F, I was able to not only understand why I failed that test, but to also use it as an opportunity to learn Math much better, at a deeper level, which opened new opportunities for me and literally changed my life. I don't remember much of what we studied in History, even though I always had A's. It was sufficient knowledge at the time, but never knowledge in depth. My Math's "misfortune," on the other hand, provided the opportunity for deep understanding and a solid base. It gave me much greater growth than I would have had without the F.

Could I have done anything to change the original F? Not really. It was done. It was in the past. I had lost my straight A-track record. Yet, the lost straight A's created the new story of a much better future track record. Even though sometimes things may seem like irreversible misfortunes, they carry the potential for something much greater, which is in unison with one or more desires in your life. Sometimes they are more general in nature, similar to my Math experience. My F didn't transform into A. But it transformed my general academic experience. And if it wasn't for my Mom's guidance into befriending the Math subject, I could have started feeling like a victim because I was given a test much harder than what we were prepared for. I could have started blaming everybody around me, including my teacher. I could have lost my confidence. In those cases, the potential of the other side of the whole, the potential that I became a success at Math, would not have realized itself. The subject of Math would have made me smaller, instead of bigger. It would have trickled down to other areas of my life. Instead, I activated a subject in a more vivid way and allowed it to expand into something more than I could have envisioned. What would have happened if I never got the F? I would have continued to do a satisfactory work in Math, but would never go beyond that. There would have been no reason for more. No desire. The F became a catalyst for me to make Math my friend, when it could have easily become the catalyst to make me hate Math forever and view it as a bitter enemy.

And now is the time to introduce to you my favorite teacher. He's only 3 inches tall, smokes hookah, and likes to hang out on top of mushrooms. If you've read "Alice in Wonderland," you've probably recognized whom I'm talking about: The Caterpillar!

While Alice was roaming in Wonderland, she kept finding things to eat that made her either smaller, or bigger. She had just eaten something that had made her 3 inches tall and urgently needed to find something else to eat to make her bigger again. That's when she came across The Caterpillar, sitting on a mushroom, leisurely smoking its hookah. The Caterpillar revealed a secret to her that made the big difference:

" 'One side will make you grow taller, and the other side will make you grow shorter.'

'One side of WHAT? The other side of WHAT?' thought Alice to herself.

'Of the mushroom,' said the Caterpillar, just as if she had asked it aloud; and in another moment it was out of sight." [10]

When you are still on the unwanted side of a subject, you can perceive it as your enemy, or as your friend. One perspective will make you smaller; the other bigger. If you focus on the unwanted with fear through mind-immobilizer eyes, it will make you smaller. It will suck greatness and life out of you. If you focus on a subject with real eyes and appreciate it for what it really is - a springboard for growth – the subject will make you bigger, and bring you to new levels of personal growth. It could be personal growth in any area: health, finances, romance, relationships, social network, creativity, personal expression, being a great parent, or having a great mind. When there are things in your life that you don't want, they are not there to kill you or torture you. They are gifts that activate a subject. They have the potential to give you growth proportionate to the strength of your desire. They can give you new power, similar to the way spinach gives Popeye a boost and in turn, Popeye gives spinach sales a boost.

The unwanted and the wanted are like a problem and a solution: you can't have a solution without a problem. They are part of the same subject. When you eat from the mushroom side that makes you grow, the wanted soon starts unfolding. When you eat from the side that makes you smaller, you stay in the unwanted. Some people call this acceptance. Only when you accept your current circumstances and stop kicking against them, are you able to move toward what you actually want. This doesn't mean that when you accept where you are, you are not going to want to move forward. If your current reality is something that you need to change, the desire is still there, whether you voice it or not. Acceptance means that you stop trying to control what you can't control and put your resources to what you can. By kicking against the current circumstances, you are not accomplishing anything. You can't change the past that resulted into the present moment. But you can change your perception of the circumstances, befriend them, and start growing bigger. Embrace the whole subject, rather than splitting it into two parts and condemning one of them.

A messy closet that makes you feel uncomfortable is good! It you make the closet subject your friend, it will give you great closet ideas and shelf innovations. It will also keep growing, branching into other things in your life that need organizing and sorting out. It will expand to clearing the clutter in your house and in your mind. A messy closet is not a bad thing, even if you don't want it! And the only way to get rid of it is to befriend it and stop trying to kick it out of your life. As a result, it will never leave your life. Instead, it will transform. It will become its opposite - a beautifully organized closet.

The unwanted is the necessary beginning, because without it, there is no desire. A subject remains either dormant, or active in the background where it doesn't get much of your attention. The unwanted activates the subject and puts it in the foreground. At this point, only the unwanted is active. The wanted hasn't realized itself yet, but the whole wants to reach its completion and transform itself to what you want. Once the wanted comes to realization, you have what you want: But there is more. You have changed. You have gone through transformation that made you bigger than you were before.

This is the desire progression:

1.   You find something in your life that you no longer want. It is the first step in the realization of what you want. Without it, a subject is not active and there is nothing to propel change.

2.   You provide a good mind environment for the unfolding of what you want. This affects your attitude that will now point toward what you want. Good mind environment is one without chronic mind immobilizers. The emotional peace is the second step of the creation of what you want.

3.   Your attitude starts affecting your thoughts and actions. You are inspired to doing things that will take you to your final destination.

4.   Depending on how big or small the journey is, you grow. Your mind environment, attitude, and inspired actions have helped you to become a new you who can now see the results in your life. This is where you get what you want.

You may ask, what about all the people who have desires that never came true? Well, they ate from the side of the mushroom that made them smaller on the subject. They practiced mind immobilizer thoughts and made the subject the enemy. We all do on many subjects in our lives. I do it too. Then, I remind myself that I have to embrace the whole and trust that nothing has gone wrong. That I haven't made a mistake or failed, that it is all perfect and everything will unfold perfectly if I get out of my own way and release the mind immobilizing thoughts. It's not always easy. When I fall, I try to get back on my feet as soon as I can. I remind myself again and again that my perception is what drives it all. And I try to make as many subjects my friends as I can. My brain soon starts to see that challenges are not my enemy. They are my biggest assets.

"When I understand my enemy well enough to defeat him, then in this moment, I also love him."

E. Wiggin

The Strength of Your Desire

Each of your desires varies in strength. For example, I go to hot yoga regularly. Among other benefits from yoga, I want to improve my flexibility. It's an existing desire. Yet, the potency of that desire is not that great. I am not motivated enough for it because I haven't felt any major discomfort about not having great flexibility. Sure, I want to look better in class, like one of those girls in the front row that everybody secretly hates, but really, how big is my necessity to have it fulfilled? Because it is just a mild desire, I do a mild job in obtaining it. And, even though it would feel great to tie my legs in a knot and put my pictures on Facebook, it's nothing that my life experience has generated a very strong desire for.

Now a strong desire I did have began on a cold January night in 2001. Then, I was living in post-communist Bulgaria. The temperature outside was about 10F and I had no money to pay for heat, let alone anything else, so the temperature inside my apartment was a little above freezing. Those days, I would look at all the buildings around me with hundreds of windows lit in the night. People were happily watching TV, while I had no TV. People were having dinners together and laughing, while I had no family to laugh with; sometimes, I wouldn't even have dinner.

During those hard times, my desires for improvement grew bigger and bigger. Life was adding fuel to them and, unlike my mild desire for better flexibility, the desire for a more successful life was a real-time wish that was ready to burst out into creation as soon as I was ready to provide the right conditions for it. That's why now my life is successful, but my body is not more flexible. One desire was generated by life itself by means of a greater discomfort, while the other was generated just by the wish to look better in class. Does it mean that I will never be more flexible? Does it mean that if your life is not bad enough to give you a strong desire for free, you won't get the improvement that you wished for?

Absolutely not: You can increase the power of desire any time you wish. But before you can jump on the gas pedal and rev up your desire, you need to fully understand the other two components: your attitude and the beliefs that you hold on the subject.

When you focus on a possible life that you could be living, you are preparing your mind to accept an alternate reality. A reality where you can live in a big house and drive a car with a sticker "My other car is a Porsche too." If you focus on it regularly, your mind becomes familiar with this alternate reality and you may become more acutely aware of the fact that you drive a clunker instead of that Porsche. Because of the difference between your current reality and the now familiar alternate life that you could live, your desire is starting to generate power.

Let me use another example.

When I was living back in communism, communism was all I knew. If someone from a free country had come to visit me back then, they would have probably felt very bad for me for all the limitations of that system, because they would have known the difference between the life I had and the life that other people were living in the free world. They would have felt bad for what they knew was a possible life of freedom that I wasn't living. From their perspective, they would see the difference. Yet, I wasn't unhappy about communism. It was all that I knew! There was no other alternate reality that my mind was familiar with. There was no discomfort relative to the fact that I was living in a communist country. The strength of my desire for living in the free world was close to zero.

But if I had met a visitor and the visitor told me stories of how they lived in the free world and showed me pictures of all the wonderful things out there, my focus would shift. I would start paying attention to the fact that I couldn't go on a trip to the Western world or that I have no chance to read books or watch movies that haven't passed the communist censure. My attention would be more and more drawn to the fact that information is very limited and that there are much better things to have than the bleak, boring merchandise in our stores. The more I focus on those daily reminders of what I don't have, the stronger my desire for freedom would be.

The strength of the desire increases when your mind recognizes the two realities: the possible future one and the current one that you are living. But it's not only the knowing that something better exists out there. It's the continuous focus that adds the power. That's why life situations do the job best. Because you almost have no choice but be focused on what is going on in your life.

A strong desire supported by attitude and belief will take you on a speedway to what you want. A strong desire that is not supported by attitude and belief will stress you out, wear you out, and send you on never ending instant gratification seeking missions.

Wanted or Unwanted? Where Your Attitude Is

A lot of modern vehicles use TPMS - Tire Pressure Monitoring System. The system allows you to check the tire pressure, and to pick out the problematic tire before it becomes hazardous. Nature gave us a similar system. I call it MIMS - Mind Immobilizer Measuring System. It reports the presence of mind immobilizers, how much the mind immobilizers have deflated your strength and which specific subject has been affected the most. The MIMS is your emotions.

When your mind is at its weakest, you feel depressed. Nothing is fun, nothing matters, in fact, you don't even want to get out of bed. When your mind is at its strongest (mind immobilizer free), it is powerful. You know who you are. You know your worth. You are solid in your stands. You know your potential. There is nothing that you can't do. Your mind is clear. Your heart is at peace. You are contented. You can create anything and you know it.

Your predominant every-day emotions will tell you if you have chronic mind immobilizers. The subjects that trigger the most negative emotions are the ones where the strongest mind-immobilizers are located.

Psychologists have created ways to place the emotions in different charts and tables to represent them in terms of different dimensions, such as emotions related to the future, emotions related to events, emotions related to self-esteem, or socially related emotions. There are two dimensions that will measure the strength of your emotional state relative to a desire: your desire strength and your mind strength.

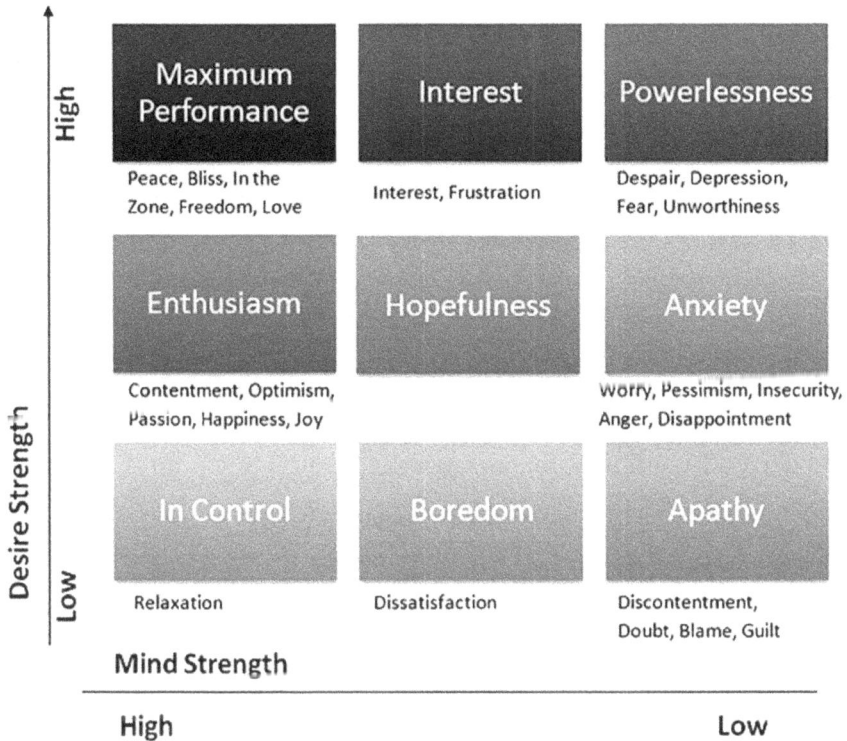

Maximum Performance	Interest	Powerlessness
Peace, Bliss, In the Zone, Freedom, Love	Interest, Frustration	Despair, Depression, Fear, Unworthiness
Enthusiasm	Hopefulness	Anxiety
Contentment, Optimism, Passion, Happiness, Joy		Worry, Pessimism, Insecurity, Anger, Disappointment
In Control	Boredom	Apathy
Relaxation	Dissatisfaction	Discontentment, Doubt, Blame, Guilt

Mind Strength

High   Low

Emotional Strength Scale

[8]

As you can see in the chart, a weak mind will keep you in the areas of apathy, blame, pessimism, anxiety and depression. You are in healing mode. A strong mind will keep you in control, relaxed, excited, feeling blissful and give you a willingness to succeed. You are in growth mode.

Let's open that closet door again and see how your mind strength can affect the desire for an organized closet.

Strong Mind:

If the closet rearrangement is not a particularly strong desire, you are in control. You take the necessary steps and it's done. No fanfares. If you have looked at magazines and got some cool ideas, the desire to rearrange the closet is stronger and now you are excited and enthusiastic, focused, in the present moment—nothing other than the closet creation matters in that moment.

In either case, the physical manifestation of the organized closet happens naturally and quickly.

Weak Mind:

If the closet rearrangement is not a strong desire, you are apathetic. The clutter bothers you, but who cares. It doesn't matter anyway. If you are really bothered by the clutter, meaning that your desire for an organized closet is stronger, you may start feeling guilty, disappointed with yourself yet again, feeling unworthy and depressed every time you think of the closet.

Your emotions give you real time feedback of the presence of mind immobilizers and how much they've weakened your current state of mind. They also give you real time feedback on how strong your mind is relative to a desire. They give you valuable data on how much you are pointed toward the wanted or toward the unwanted. Knowing this is power! If you feel powerless or depressed, it is not the end of the world. MIMS tells you which thoughts need changing. You will learn how to do deal with such habits in Part 2.

MIMS can also be represented vertically. Each of us has a predominant place on the chart that is our default range. The chart below is a general guideline used to illustrate the idea of the mind's default position up and down the various states of strength.

High	Peace, Bliss, In the Zone, Freedom, Love, Maximum Performance (no active mind immobilizers)
	Contentment, Optimism, Enthusiasm, Happiness, Joy (few to no active mind immobilizers)
	Relaxation, In Control (few to no active mind immobilizers)
Mind Strength	Hopefulness (few active mind immobilizers)
	Interest, Frustration (a few active mind immobilizers)
	Boredom, Dissatisfaction (more active mind immobilizers)
	Apathy, Discontentment, Doubt, Blame, Guilt (chronically active mind immobilizers)
	Worry, Anxiety, Pessimism, Insecurity, Anger, Disappointment (chronically active mind immobilizers)
Low	Despair, Depression, Powerlessness, Fear, Unworthiness (mind immobilizer "infection")

[8]

It's important to remember that it's okay not to be strong in every subject. Even the most successful people in the world have subjects they are weak in. Professional athletes may have physical success, but perhaps they're weak at math. J.K. Rowling is strong at writing and creative thinking, but maybe she's terrible when it comes to directions. Each person has subjects they naturally excel at and subjects that they don't. You can still manifest your desires in your strong subjects, even while you're still going through the process of getting rid of your mind immobilizers in your weaker subjects.

Let's relate the chart to the basics of the desire. A strong mind will naturally point your attitude to success. A mind that habitually points toward the unwanted end of the subject is usually a mind that is weakened by mind immobilizers. A strong mind is not achieved by doing something to make it strong. It is achieved by stopping doing what makes it weak. In other words, you will need to go on a mind-immobilizer-free diet.

The good news is if you start changing your emotions, over time, it increases your mind strength. That's why it is important to do a general mind immobilizer cleanup. On one level, it helps you to resolve the negative emotions and move to a happier place. This naturally increases your mind strength. On another level, it resolves mind immobilizers, even deeply rooted ones.

In the (Manifesting) Zone

To manifest a desire, you need to have a disturbance in your life. If you are thirsty, you want a glass of water. Thirsty is the disturbance: water is the desire. So you make a conscious effort of getting up, going to the kitchen, and getting the glass of water. Desire manifested, desire realized. For a bigger desire, like starting a successful business, when the desire is born, it disturbs the balance of your life. This disturbance is the motivation for you to go out there and do what needs to be done to succeed. If your mind is strong, you will be persistent, focused, stable, and you soon see results. If your mind is weak, the imbalance will increase and show itself in states characterized by more negative emotions.

For more challenging desires, the process is accompanied by emotional and mental growth. It's like when you were growing up and your parents bought you clothes that were slightly bigger so that you could grow into them. It is not that you manifested clothes that fit you. You grew into the clothes and they fit you. The same goes for your mental environment. Your desires are the clothes your parents bought you. Right now, they're too big, but if you remain self-aware and focus toward the wanted desire, you will soon have a mental environment big enough to wear the desire you want comfortably. The ability to make the desire come true was always inside you. You changed. You became bigger.

The process of moving from a disturbed state to a balanced one is the fun part of life! Think about it: the time between being little and being an adult had good times and adventures. Would you trade all those experiences for instantaneous growth into an adult size? The growth is where the journey happens. It is where you change: For you to have what you want, you have to change and become a new, expanded you. In a way, we are mid-way on a journey, all the time. We constantly have new desires, many of them at the same time. There will never be a time when everything is accomplished. In this way, we are always in the process of journeying. And this is where all the wonderful experiences happen. When you go for a hike, it's not like the hike is about reaching the end point. It's the enjoyment of the movement and the exploration of the beauty around that makes it special. Reaching the end point is the excuse for the journey and the fun on the way. The moment we reach the goal, our desire toward the goal diminishes and our excitement, as well as our drive, subsides.

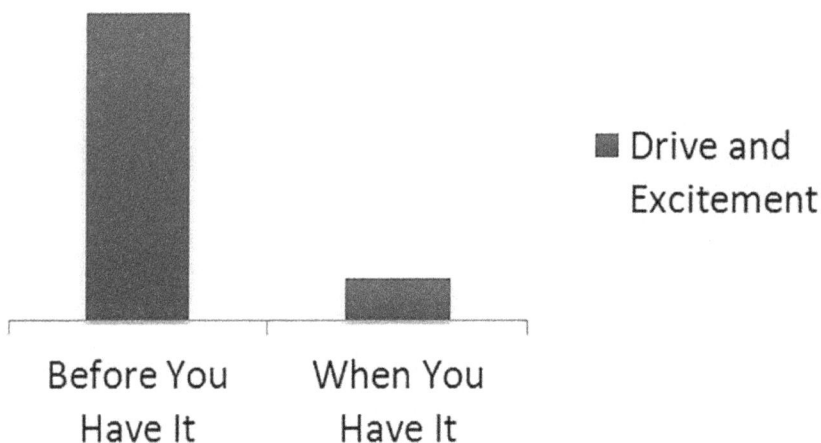

Before You Have It   When You Have It

Drive and Excitement

If we are constantly having desires and some of them have not reached their completion yet, does it mean that we are constantly running around in a disturbed, "thirsty" state? Isn't that bad? Doesn't it create stress?

There are two types of stress. Let's call them good stress and bad stress. Good stress is something that you need. It is the motivational force that keeps you moving. It is the drive that keeps you going toward your goals and desires. It is the slightly disturbed, "thirsty" state that happens when you come up with a desire and stays there until the goal is reached. It is also known as Eustress: positive stress. Without it, you can't focus your attention.

The thing is, it has to be just the right amount of stress. Too little will not be enough to motivate you. You may feel bored, apathetic, or uninterested. Add a little more than necessary and you have the bad stress - worry, anxiety, nervousness, or fear. The right amount makes the difference between being under stimulated, properly stimulated (what every lady needs), or over stimulated. Psychologists use the term "arousal level" to describe how stimulated you are at any given moment. If your desire is not strong enough, you may not be motivated enough to do anything about it, so you're under stimulated. If your desire is strong, but you have too many mind immobilizers that increase the stress, you become over stimulated. You are eating from the mushroom side that makes you smaller and you get real-time feedback by the way you feel through your MIMS, your emotions.

When the stimulation is just right, you are in the zone. You are relaxed and highly focused. Mental energies are flowing freely. Challenges and mind strengths are in balance and you feel more powerful than usual. Doing what you are doing becomes not means to an end, but something that is worth doing for its own sake. Directing your attention in such state is practically effortless. You are growing bigger.

Two men, Robert M. Yerkes, PhD, and John D. Dodson, PhD introduced the inverted U curve in 1908. It represents the different states of under stimulation, perfect stimulation and overstimulation. Here's the chart:

Now let's see how this chart relates to real life. [11]

For your desire to manifest, you need to be in a "thirsty" state: You have to be stimulated enough to want a change. You also need to reduce the mind immobilizing habits, so that you don't go into over stimulation where your attention is brought into the unwanted. Being in the manifesting zone relative to a desire is not a constant state: It is a balancing act that requires your conscious adjustment.

If you are not motivated enough, you need to increase the strength of your desire. Think about what you want and why you want it. Imagine yourself having it. Remember, focus adds fuel to the desire. Get inspired.

If you know that your desire is strong but you feel negative emotions when you think about it, including being jealous of others who have it, you have mind immobilizers that put you in over stimulation. You will need to resolve the conflicting thoughts. The next part of the book will teach you how to control the mind immobilizers.

Use your MIMS and the Emotional Strength Scale to give you real time feedback.

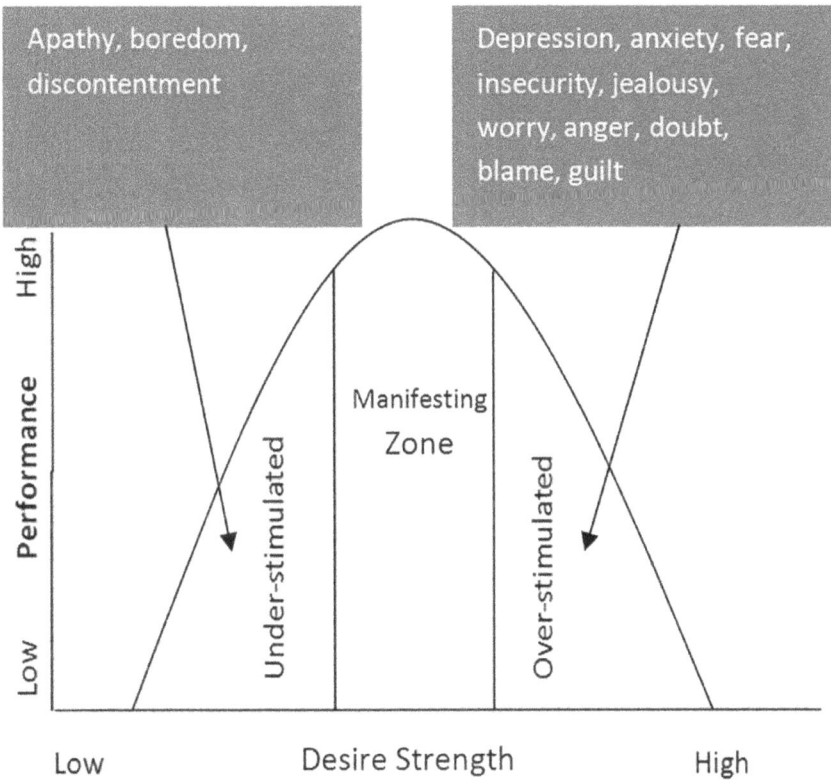

Apathy, boredom, discontentment		Depression, anxiety, fear, insecurity, jealousy, worry, anger, doubt, blame, guilt

Performance (High / Low) vs **Desire Strength** (Low / High)

Manifesting Zone

Under-stimulated

Over-stimulated

When you are adjusting the strength of your desire, keep in mind that the stronger the desire, the more skillful you need to be in controlling the mind immobilizers. It's like riding a horse - the faster the ride, the better you need to be at balancing. As you can see in the Emotional Strength Scale, stronger desires coupled with mind immobilizers produce more intense negative emotions. At the same time, a strong desire with no mind immobilizer puts you in higher performance states and a speedway to your goal.

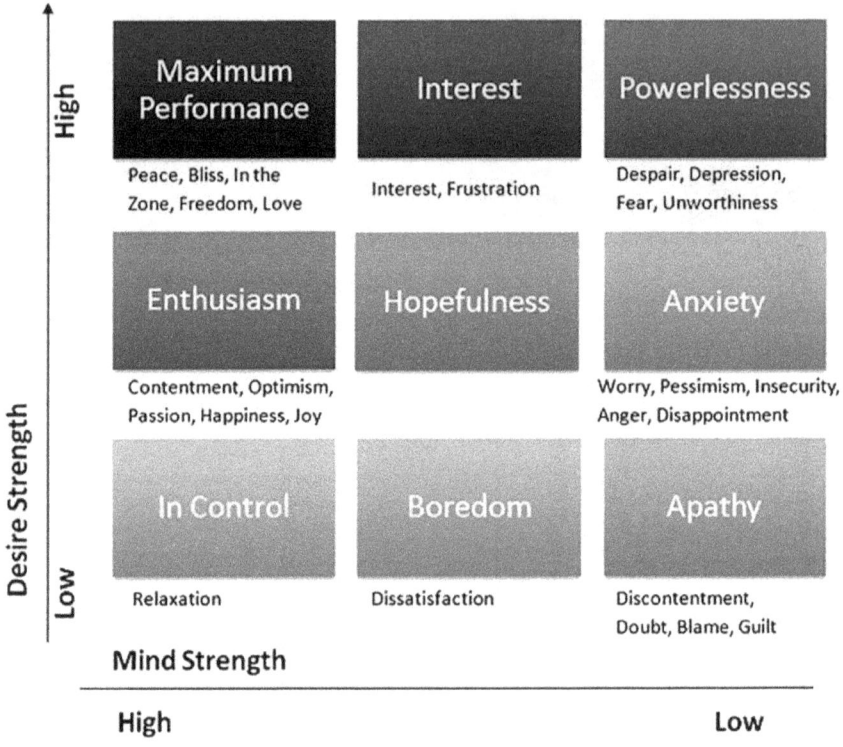

		Mind Strength
Maximum Performance Peace, Bliss, In the Zone, Freedom, Love	**Interest** Interest, Frustration	**Powerlessness** Despair, Depression, Fear, Unworthiness
Enthusiasm Contentment, Optimism, Passion, Happiness, Joy	**Hopefulness**	**Anxiety** Worry, Pessimism, Insecurity, Anger, Disappointment
In Control Relaxation	**Boredom** Dissatisfaction	**Apathy** Discontentment, Doubt, Blame, Guilt

Desire Strength — High / Low

Mind Strength — High / Low

Emotional Strength Scale

The Shower Phenomenon

Have you ever struggled to get a thought out, only to have that "aha!" moment later, in the shower? By stepping away from the problem, the solution comes to you. When you hop into the shower, you are relaxing, perfectly stimulated (you can make your own joke here), and you get a brilliant idea or solution! Most people know about this fun fact. They call it, "clearing your head." We know that what's really happening is that we're ridding ourselves of Fixed Thinking.

Let me give you two puzzles where people normally miss the answer, due to fixed thinking:

How many animals of each kind did Moses bring on the Ark?

Most people answer quickly: two animals of each kind. This common mistake happens because the solution comes from the framework "how many animals of each kind," completely ignoring the obvious fact that Moses didn't bring any animals on the Ark. It was Noah.

The second puzzle is more complicated and it may take a little longer time to solve. You have two rooms - Room A and Room B. In Room A, there are three light switches: Switch 1, Switch 2, and Switch 3. They are all in "Off" position. In Room B, there is only one old fashioned light bulb hanging from the ceiling. The rest of the room is empty. You are in Room A. Once you leave Room A, you can't go back. By pressing the switches in Room A, how can you determine with 100% accuracy which switch turns on and off the light bulb in Room B?

If you want to think about it, you can skip this paragraph and come back for the answer later. Most people try to find different combinations of turning the switches on or off. However, three switches are one too many to determine with 100% accuracy. One more factor is needed. That factor is outside the box. If you paid attention, the puzzle is about an old fashioned light bulb. What happens when an old fashioned light bulb has been on for a while? It heats up. And this is the third factor that solves the puzzle. Here's the solution: you turn Switch 1 on and wait for a few minutes (however long it takes for a light bulb to get recognizably warmer). You turn Switch 1 off and turn Switch 2 on. You leave the room and go into Room 2. If the light bulb is on, the answer is Switch 2. If the light bulb is off and it's warm, it is Switch 1. If the light bulb is off and it's cold, it is Switch 3.

These two puzzles demonstrate that the answers could often be missed when approached from a preset framework of mind. Once you step out of that box, you are opening yourself for the unlimited potential of ideas and possibilities.

Let's relate this to a desire. If you have a lot of mind immobilizing thoughts relative to a desire, they are not only pointing you to the unwanted, but they also create a framework approach to the possible solution that limits the scope of possibilities within itself.

If we go back to the example of you wanting to grow a successful business, some of the mind immobilizing thoughts may be that it is risky, that you are fearful about investing time and efforts into something that may fail, that you've tried it before and it didn't work, or that you are not good enough to be successful. How many brilliant ideas can shine through such framework? And even if you are at the right place at the right time to meet a key person for your business venture, you may completely miss that opportunity because your perception is clouded through the limitation of the mind immobilizer framework. Your manifesting experience is completely governed by the framework through which you perceive the world.

In this next part of the book, we are about to "hop into the shower" to "clear your head" of the mind immobilizing habits. It will help you to remove a lot of the fixed thinking that prevents you from seeing the solutions, as well as to release your hold on the unwanted, so that you can start unleashing your potential. In the process, you will start remembering your happier, creative, confident self that is excited about life and knows your power.

Part 2: Clearing the Mind Immobilizers

Somebody Needs to Be in Charge

You saw how your behavior is made up of conditioned responses and established pathways. You saw how your brain wants to protect you and engages different processes to ensure your survival, even if they are not always beneficial for your goals. Now, you need to put somebody in charge. You need to assign a manager. And there's no one better qualified than You.

Let's say that you have decided to have a relaxing evening at home. You light the candles in your living room, pour a glass of nice wine, turn your favorite soothing music on and sink into your favorite recliner. Bliss! You look at your candles, and your mind wanders to the first date you had with your ex. That reminds you about the failed relationship, the disappointments, the broken promises. You replay the past like a movie, which you decide to abandon, because it's not really helping your relaxation plans. No worries! You move onto how great this idea was. Maybe you'll make every Wednesday a Relaxation Wednesday. You think maybe you'll go to a wholesale store to stock up on good wine. Yes, good wine with candles at home is a great habit to build. Maybe change the décor to enhance the ambience. That might be fun. Maybe even invite friends! Mary and John. No, Mary just won't shut up. How could a person talk so much! Oh, blue throw pillows is just what you need right now. You could get those when you stock up on wine.

The thing is, while you are jumping from thought to thought, daydreaming about the future and the past, you've already finished your glass of wine. But you can hardly remember drinking it. Your mind was far away. While your focus was elsewhere, you weren't present to enjoy your relaxation in the moment.

You may have heard the expression "monkey-mind." It represents the idea that the mind is hard to tame and it likes to stay busy, so it plays movies, which take on the form of past experience, future daydreams, or just plain random thoughts. Why is that?

The brain has two modes of operation, each of which uses different brain regions. The first mode is the "monkey-mind" mode, the mode you were in on Relaxation Wednesday. This "monkey" or "idle" mode is when the brain is weaving a story that involves you, the people around you, your past and your future. This mode does not require a lot of resources to run and therefore it is an easy, low effort activity. We do it all day long.

The other mode of operation is the direct experience operation. Remember when you first sat in the recliner after you poured yourself the glass of your favorite wine? For a few moments in time, you were focused on the comfort of the recliner, the flavor of the wine, the sounds of the music, and the ambience of the candles. The direct experience mode puts your focus into the present moment. You are mindful of what is going on in real time in the world around you, as well as your inner world. Direct experience may be the sensations of the ambiance of a relaxing evening, a mantra in a meditation, the taste of the food in your mouth, or simply observing that the brain is playing a story. You switch between these two modes all the time, but most people tend to predominantly stay in "idle" mode. The direct experience mode is a lot harder to sustain for longer periods of time. Sometimes even half a minute is too hard to do! It requires a lot more effort. If you want to put this to test, try to focus on the sensations in your right hand for at least 20 seconds. You will notice that it is hard to stay fully focused and present even for 20 seconds. [9]

Your "idle" brain is not much different from an online movie store like "Netflix" or "Amazon." Based on your prior choices and habits, it puts in the foreground movies that the system thinks you may like. The movies you play the most shape your mental environment. Your mental environment in turn shapes your attitude and affects your manifestations. Even though some movies are common for your idle brain to run, they may be creating a mental environment that is not beneficial for what you want. They are solidifying networks that may be standing in your way and sabotaging your desires.

Being able to make the difference between your idle mode and your direct experience mode will help you understand when you are and aren't focusing on the real world fully, and become more selective in the stories you engage in and cultivate new habits of movie watching: movies of appreciation, strength, and happy endings.

Somebody told me a great story once. John is working in his garage when his hammer handle breaks. He really wants to finish the job fast, so he decides to go and ask his neighbor George to lend him his hammer. As he is walking to George's house, he is thinking:

"Well, I'm gonna ask him for a hammer, but when he sees me, he will remember the time when I asked him for his drill. He will probably get frustrated with me for asking him for things. When he gets frustrated, he will look at me in his way, like it's my fault that my hammer broke. He'll probably say: "Why don't you go to the store to buy your own hammer, instead of asking for my things all the time!" When he starts talking to me like that, it will drive me crazy! If I had the time, of course I would go to the store! It's not like I am asking for something huge here, it's just a hammer! What's the big deal! In fact, I don't want his hammer! I don't want anything from him! I'm not gonna put up with his attitude!" As John's thinking this, he arrives at George's door. When George opens the door, John says:

"I don't want your drill, I don't want your hammer, I don't want anything of yours! Go get a life!"

Your idle brain not only shapes your mental climate, but it often primes your decisions and actions in real life. The brain may weave a story based on prior experience and interpretations that has little to do with reality. Yet, you may be prompted to decisions based on the story priming.

The two modes of operation usually exclude each other. When you were sitting in the recliner and the mental movies started, you lost the vividness of your physical senses. It works both ways. If you are deep into a movie that is not that great, all you have to do is focus on direct experience, like mindfully taking a few deep breaths. Once you look at the movie from the perspective of an observer, not a character in it, you see it for what it is - a story your brain is weaving based on the data that it holds. Another way to interrupt a movie is by simply recognizing that your brain is playing a movie. The moment you become aware of what's happening in real time, you switch from "idle" mode to "direct experience" mode.

Consciously and mindfully switching from idle mode to direct experience teaches you to direct your focus at will and strengthens your attention "muscle." It teaches you to recognize patterns, so that you can fine-tune your attitude at will. If you practice being mindful through direct experience, you are actually changing the structure of your brain. Studies show that it thickens regions that are involved with cognitive control and directing of attention. You are building a new mental environment.

Now that you understand the two operational modes, you have created a verbal picture of them in your brain. You have created a flowchart of the process. Having a verbal picture of what is going on in your brain is enough to start widespread changes. Having the language for what is going on in the brain not only normalizes the experience, but also allows you to become more sensitive to subtle changes your brain may make, so you can recognize them quicker, and make the necessary changes. This fine-tunes your ability to be in control of your brain, rather than your brain controlling your choices.

The mind immobilizers are movies that you've played a lot until they became the system's "recommendation."

As you go through the different mind immobilizers in the next chapters, understand that they are nothing more than a story that your brain is weaving based on its interpretations and stored data. By consciously switching to direct experience mode, meaning that you recognize that the brain is only playing a movie, you can become selective of the stories that you play in your mind. You can recognize what character you are stepping into and change it willfully. If you play a victim, you will never be a hero until you change your mindset. If you're punishing the bad guys in your mind stories, you can evaluate the reasons why: maybe it's triggered by guilt, or blame, or feeling unworthy. You can start playing more inspirational movies, movies of success, or just movies of appreciation and gratitude. By doing that, you are changing your mental environment. By changing the environment consciously, you are taking charge. You are becoming an environ-mentalist. Once you start changing your mind environment, the changes on one subject influence others and they reinforce each other.

Worry

There are many things that I am not good at: way too many to list here. But there is one thing that I used to be really good at—worrying. Worrying about things was such a big part of my life that when I sensed a moment when I had no worry, I would immediately get very worried that something is out of normal and wrong. I didn't know any better. Hey, I come from a long line of worriers! I was so good at worrying that I had successfully trained my mind to cover every possible bad thing that could happen and see no peace until I had a confirmation that none of them had come to pass. Talk about a high demand task!

I later discovered that I had developed OCD - Obsessive Compulsive Disorder. There is a lot to be said about OCD, but in short, it is the inability of the brain to switch away from any worrisome thought. Instead, it obsessively cycles to that thought over and over, regardless of logic or reasoning. I was worried about my loved ones, I was worried about my home catching on fire, I was worried if I locked the door before I left, and I repeatedly checked it again and again, never trusting my memory that I did. I had an answering machine at home, which for most people means seeing how many people still know they have a home phone. For me, my answering machine had other purposes.

Here are two facts: 1. For an answering machine to work, it needs to be plugged into an electrical outlet. 2. If a home catches on fire, the electricity shuts down. Do you see what I'm getting at? I could call home when I was gone and if the answering machine came on, I knew that everything at home was all right, so I could switch my worries to other, more important things. I had perfected the worrying!

Worrying was like living in chains. When I saw this mind immobilizer for what it really was, I was able to set myself free from the chains I had set for myself. Understanding and facing my worry is what set me free.

Your worries may not be as extreme as mine were. Regardless, they are still taking your energy, your resources, and your brilliance. Every worry is one more brick in a house that you have to get out of.

Worry and Your Mind

When you worry, you are immobilizing yourself from doing anything enjoyable or constructive in the most important moment that you have in life - now. I have gone through many of those dark moments of being completely paralyzed by worry about what could happen. When I look back, none of those worries ever became a reality, but I missed on many precious moments that I could have enjoyed and a lot of opportunities that I could have jumped on. It kept me from realizing my potential and following my dreams. If you could go back in time in a moment when you were paralyzed by worry, what would you tell yourself?

Here's the absurdity of worry: it is an attempt to control what you can't control. When you worry, you perceive that something in your world is endangered. This, in turn, activates the fight-or-flight response to a smaller or greater degree. If you do it chronically, three things happen: your immune system suffers, your brain suffers, and your power in the present moment is greatly reduced, due to the inhibition of your prefrontal cortex. You also may become irritable, fearful, angry, or disinterested, all emotional responses to the fight-or-flight reaction. All negative emotional responses, as your MIMS would tell you.

Imagine your attention as a nozzle with two settings - jet and shower. The same amount of water goes through on each setting, but the power of the water stream is different. When you worry, instead of focusing your attention deliberately, it is dispersed between the current activity and all the worries that you are maintaining at that moment. In other words, you are operating in shower setting: the same resources are used, but without much power. On the other hand, if you reduce the worries, your attention is operating at the jet setting: a powerfully focused mind that you can use to grow your talents and explore your full potential.

Worrying about Others

Even though we are taught that it is a good thing to worry about the ones we love, worry is not an indication of love. Worry is an attempt to secure the wellbeing of the relationship in a way that we want it to be, but in reality it only limits its potential and full expression. Everybody has the right to be what he or she chooses without any conditions set by the other. Worrying about others is an attempt to control what you can't control.

When you worry about somebody, the underlying message is that you don't trust that they can live and handle their life for themselves, or that outside forces can invade their experience and something bad could happen to them. In a way, you self-promote yourself to the position of Manager of the World and attempt to handle processes and events that are not your job, your responsibility, or your right to manage. You don't have those qualifications, plus, trust me, you don't want the job anyway - imagine the daily to-do list and the knowledge that is required! So quit it!

When you worry about somebody, you also project the message that things could always go very wrong and instead of empowering them, this message brings their focus to unwanted outcomes. Your worry could make their focus weaker and increase their own self-doubt and worry. It could also scatter their attention in trying to soothe your fears while maintaining their own life balance. Wouldn't you want your loved ones to be stable and strong, instead of diminishing their power by introducing doubt and fear? In some cases, you may go as far as trying to prevent them from doing what is dear and important to them for fear that something bad could happen.

Similar to the way that you are now taking steps to build a strong mind and try to overcome the hurdles of all the worries that others introduced in your life, the best way to help somebody else is to empower them to believe in their own strengths and potential. From an empowered state of mind, even if they fall, they can stand back on their feet stronger from the experience, and quickly move to the solution. Worry will not secure your loved ones' safety or success. Helping them to trust their own abilities will.

Let me illustrate this with a story. I was driving to see a friend out of town one night. As soon as I started going up the mountain, a snow blizzard started and the road conditions became scary. While on the road, I called and said that he shouldn't worry, that I was on my way and if I needed help, I would call. He said: "I wasn't worried. I know that you know what you are doing."

There was no visibility and I had to use my GPS to make sure that I was staying on the road. I was scared. I couldn't see anything, but his words were like a guiding light that kept me on the road that night. I kept repeating his words and they empowered me: "I know that you know what you are doing." If he could trust me that I knew what I was doing, shouldn't I trust myself too?

Worrying about somebody is not an indication of love. In fact, true love is unconditional. It doesn't require conformity to your idea of how their life should be or how they should choose. If you love somebody and you want the best for them, find a way to empower them, so they can explore their potential and growth. Which is exactly the opposite of what worry does.

I want to share a wonderful quote from one of my favorite writers, Paulo Coelho:

Tell your heart that the fear of suffering is worse than the suffering itself. And that no heart has ever suffered when it goes in search of its dreams, because every second of the search is a second's encounter with God and with eternity.

Wouldn't you want this for your loved ones? Wouldn't you want to inspire and empower them? Wouldn't you want them to say one day, "Because of you, I didn't give up!"

I saw a really good flowchart that somebody created and posted on Facebook. I don't know their name, so I will call them Unknown Genius. It goes like this:

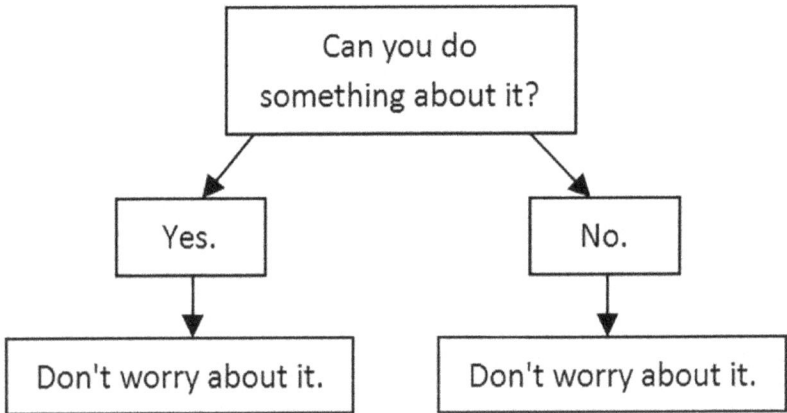

```
              ┌─────────────────────┐
              │      Can you do      │
              │  something about it? │
              └─────────────────────┘
                  ↙              ↘
         ┌──────────┐        ┌──────────┐
         │   Yes.   │        │    No.   │
         └──────────┘        └──────────┘
              ↓                    ↓
  ┌────────────────────┐  ┌────────────────────┐
  │ Don't worry about it.│  │ Don't worry about it.│
  └────────────────────┘  └────────────────────┘
```

Everybody has worries! Cut it out.

What Worry Is Not

Have you ever been inspired by something? You feel so full of life, you know your potential, you know how good you are, you know that you are able to do anything. You are not afraid of how things will happen, but you are excited about what's coming next, even if it's a challenge. The same thing happens when you stop worrying. Your body is energized, your mind is clear, your heart is at peace and you feel happy for no reason. All these feelings are moments when your energies are flowing freely without any blockages.

Could Worry Be Good?

Now that we've spent all this book real estate on explaining how bad worry is, we need to make things fair. Worry is not a villain. Sometimes, a little bit of worry may be what propels you to step out of your comfort zone and take action for a change. Instead of being a setback, it could be a springboard to propel you on your path.

How can you tell the difference?

Good worry is short-lived. It is like a push that gives you a momentum booster. It's like if your car battery died and you needed a jump. You don't need to keep the jumper cables on all day. If it is good worry, it will propel action for a change and the worry itself will subside. If it is a bad worry, it will immobilize you without any positive effects.

Chronic worries are never good. They are worries that don't cause change, but remain active, immobilizing you from unleashing your potential and reinforcing a negative mind environment. So, let me repeat the Unknown Genius flow chart:

```
            ┌─────────────────────┐
            │      Can you do     │
            │  something about it?│
            └─────────────────────┘
              ↙                 ↘
     ┌──────────┐          ┌──────────┐
     │   Yes.   │          │   No.    │
     └──────────┘          └──────────┘
          ↓                     ↓
┌──────────────────────┐  ┌──────────────────────┐
│ Don't worry about it.│  │ Don't worry about it.│
└──────────────────────┘  └──────────────────────┘
```

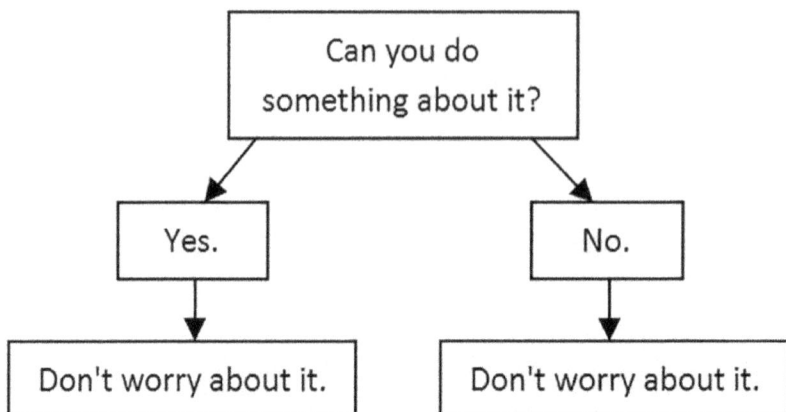

Chronic Worries Are Addictive

Being worried is no fun. I haven't heard of anybody planning to go have some worrying time, or friends getting together to worry. Worry does not change the future and it does not control the situation. There is absolutely nothing beneficial of worry. But it is a habit that is very hard to break. Why is that?

Habits are ingrained in the brain. They are automatic processes that often happen without our conscious decision to participate in the habit. As you read earlier in the book, we often leave reason and common sense behind, engaging in our habits over and over.

Worry could be a means to avoid doing what you need to do in the present moment. Worry can be the reason you avoid taking risks. Being worried about what may happen is a great excuse not to take action, even if it is an area that you want to see great accomplishments.

Worry could carry other rewards that you are unconsciously seeking. Remember how we said that the brain doesn't want you to feel bad and it looks for an activity or a substance that it thinks will make you feel better? Your brain has built the link between worrying and immediate reward and would often guide you to worry in an attempt to reach the reward. If you are trying to quit smoking, for example, you may start looking for things to worry about to give yourself the excuse to have a smoke.

Worry may also get you attention from others. When you share your worries, they respond by trying to make you feel better. Worry gives you the opportunity to create the connection with the other person and evoke empathy, compassion, and genuine attempt to help.

Lastly, worry may just be a habit that gets initiated by specific triggers. When the trigger is present, before you can consciously evaluate the situation, your brain has already started the habit loop.

How to Stop Bad Worrying

To stop bad or chronic worrying, you have to be prepared to do some habit changing. As with anything new, you will have to be prepared to make some little baby steps out of your comfort zone. As an ex-master worrier, I know that it could be scary but when you gradually work on it, it will become easier and easier. If I could do it, you can definitely do it too.

Remember how earlier in this book we said that you are now taking a new job as a Manager? When you start worrying, you're idle brain is playing a very scary movie in your head. And most of the times, you believe that the movie is a documentary, rather than just fiction coming from your mind's interpretation. Notice the movie and recognize it as such. The very recognition that it's a fantasy puts you in direct experience mode. Train yourself to recognize the worry as a mental movie as soon as possible, before it has caught momentum. The more you do this, the easier it will get when future worries come. Don't judge yourself for worrying. Your worry is a result of many different components in your past experience. Accept that you are worried. Realize that your mind is weaving a story based on its own interpretation.

Try not to focus on the two outcomes: what you don't want to happen and what you want to happen. Allow the idea that there are unlimited outcomes, some of which you are not able to conceive of yet. Realize that by worrying, you are not controlling anything. On the contrary, you are losing your control. Remind yourself that worrying is contributing to a generally bad mind environment for your desires. Unless the worry motivates you to make changes, remind yourself that there is no benefit to it. It's like eating a horrible meal with lots of additives and no nutrition. It tastes bad, it is bad for you and it has no nutrition value. Yikes!

If the worry is intense, you may not have a clear rational. At that time, your prefrontal cortex has been asked to take a mandatory break in lieu of the fight-or-flight response. Not to worry. You can bring it back. Mental activity breaks the momentum of the fight-or-flight response and brings your prefrontal cortex back in charge. A simple mental activity is to count to 20. If that's not enough, you can count backward from 50. That's enough to stop the intensity, so that you can get your reasoning back: Enough to realize that you are playing a fantasy that has nothing to do with reality and that you can turn it off by choice. You are the Manager. And as a manager, you understand that worry is an attempt to control what you can't, which robs you of your power to control what you can.

Notice if worry is a means to a reward that you are seeking. Are you looking for an excuse to eat what you have decided not to, or have a smoke, or have somebody listen to you so you can vent? Recognizing it will help you to better understand your brain and have better control over your reactions.

Take action. Action is a great antidote to worry. Physical exercises, regardless how light they are, do an incredible job! Engaging mental activities can be very beneficial too, as long as they are more stimulating than the worrisome thoughts.

Ask yourself the question, "Am I changing anything by worrying right now?"

And lastly, start controlling the times of your worries. You may assign special times of the day when worry is permitted, like 10 minutes in the morning and 10 minutes in the afternoon. Delay your worries for those designated times. By delaying the worry, you are gaining back your power in the present moment and breaking the habit of compulsively stepping into worry. You are gaining control of the worrying habit. If that's too much to do at the beginning, you can simply delay the worry. You can start with one minute, then extend to two, then five, ten and so forth. You are training yourself to be in charge.

What Not to Do with Bad Worries

Do not try to stop the worrisome thoughts. As you will read later in the book, trying to stop a thought only makes it more persistent in the long run. Instead, use reframing, delay the thought, count from 50 backwards, recognize that your idle mind is playing a fantasy, or simply do some physical exercise, even if it is just walking.

Do not believe the worry. Remember, it's just a story that your brain is weaving.

Do not engage in rituals to prevent the bad thing from happening. Engaging in rituals only reinforces the worrying in the long run.

Do not try to justify the worry. When you are worried, your brain will come up with many different reasons why you should worry to justify the internal anxiety.

Don't try to list all the possible bad things that could happen. This makes the worry stronger. Worry is a mind immobilizer that creates a habit of thought that things can go very wrong in your life.

Guilt

Guilt and worry are very similar in the way that we stay paralyzed in the present moment by focusing into the future or the past on things that we have no control over.

Guilt is a skill that you were taught from a very early age and one you mastered throughout your life experience. We all did. Guilt is society's way of establishing a control function to make sure that every member of the social group complies with the established rules, so that the overall wellbeing of the group is secured. Since you were a child, you've been learning that there are right things to do and wrong things to do. When you do something that is wrong, you are guilty and you should stay in the feeling of guilt until further notice. Usually what relieves the guilt is an accepted apology from the affected party, fixing of the damage that you imposed, receiving forgiveness from a religious or other institutions, or performing of any ritual that is agreed upon in your social group. In most cases, though, it is an event outside yourself that relieves the guilt and if that doesn't happen, you are stuck with the guilt.

Imagine having to carry a backpack full of rocks all the time. This is how guilt weighs down on you. Each unresolved guilt feeling is one more rock in your backpack. Some rocks are so heavy that the burden becomes too much to carry. Some people break down under it. Others duly carry it on and on. But how could you navigate and keep moving in your life when you have to carry that weight on your shoulders?

We all have bought into this cycle and in a way, we've taken it to an extreme. Because feeling guilty is hard to bear, we limit our choices of action to prevent making ripples in somebody else's life that we could later on feel guilty about. We carefully select our words so as not to offend others. We will sacrifice something that is important to us so we don't hurt others' feelings. Instead of our inner compass guiding us, we let fear direct our choices. We feel undeserving of good things because there is a whole list of "bad" things we've done that we feel guilty about.

Mistakes

When you are faced with a choice, which happens many times during your day, you always make the best possible decision. Why is it the best? Because if you were able to make a better decision than the one you picked, then you would have done it. In any moment, we do the best that we are able to do. What affects your choice? Three things:

1.) All your prior moments of experience and prior mind conditioning.

2.) Your mood.

3.) The priming of your mind.

Even though it may seem that a decision is a conscious action taken in a specific moment, in reality, the options had already been long reduced down by your brain.

1.   Prior Programming

First, the available choices have to pass your mind's programming screening. Anything that conflicts with that programming is removed from the list. In the decision making process, your brain is busy making the decision for you, based on what you've learned in the past. If, for example, you see a cockroach in your sink, you have many options: You can carefully put the cockroach on a sheet of paper, making sure you don't hurt it, and gently take it outside to set it free. You can smash it in the sink. You can spray it with a bug-spray. You can pour whisky on top of it to get it drunk, so it won't escape, then grab it with a napkin, flush it down the toilet and avoid making a mess in your sink. You can start crying because things like that keep happening to you. You can call someone who can handle cockroaches. Hey, you could even Instagram the cockroach, give the roach its own page and get a thousand followers that day! The list of options could be very large.

For most people, the first and last choices are not options for them. Who would touch a cockroach, let alone Instagram it! This is because our programming tells us that cockroaches are filthy, they can multiply and infest our homes and for the most part, they are disgusting creatures.

Now, let's take the same situation, but switch the cockroach with a ladybug. Suddenly humane release into the wild or taking a picture of the ladybug become likely choices for a lot of people because ladybugs are a symbol of luck and they are generally beautiful insects. Images of ladybugs are normal in decorations, postcards and beautiful photos.

In this way, your brain makes available only the choices that it considers sensible and acceptable based on its prior programming.

2.   Your Mood

Another factor in the decision-making process that works simultaneously with the prior programming filtering is the current state of your mind, or your mood. Will you choice change, depending on how happy or sad you are at the moment? This is where it gets interesting.

Your mind is amazing in the way that it only allows you to see whatever its settings are set for. Your mood is a powerful filter that not only affects your perception of the present moment but also affects your recollection of the past.

Can you remember a time when you successfully completed a project after hours of hard work and study? In that moment of success, if you looked back at all the hurdles that you had to overcome, each of them looked like victory and success. You thought of them and felt proud. The thought of them made you feel good. This is because you were looking at the past experience through the filter of success and a state of mind of happiness. Alternatively, if your project failed and you had to start all over again, you would look at those exact same experiences and they would seem to you like really discouraging difficult problems that you had to face yet again. It's the same past, yet you view the same events in a completely different manner depending on how your mind is filtering them through your emotions. As a result, when you are faced with a choice, you use your emotions to filter out all your prior experiences in order to make the correct choice. If you are feeling inspired, you will be activating all the moments that were inspiring in your past. If you are discouraged or depressed, you filter out the happy coloring and your current choices are based on that mindset. Your bad mood is an indication that you are having a fight-or-flight response activation. In such state, you may incorrectly class people and events as threats. Your brain limits your available conscious choices accordingly.

3.   Priming

There is term in psychology called "priming." It refers to gaining sensitivity to a certain stimuli after being exposed to it.

In the University of Michigan, a psychologist named John Bargh gave a group of young people a set of words and asked them to construct sentences from them. The words were relating to elderliness, like "Florida," "Bingo," "forgetful," "wrinkle." While none of the words had a mention of slowness or speed, the young students that were primed with these words walked more slowly when exiting the testing booth than those that were primed with neutral words. Keep in mind that the word "old" was never mentioned in the experiment, but the exposure to words relating to "old" triggered a behavior typical for older age. When the students were asked later on, none of them had consciously thought of older age while constructing the sentences. These findings led to the conclusion that priming can happen automatically and influence the behavior with little or no awareness. [12]

Let's take this to a daily situation. Let's say that you've been listening to a friend complaining about the fact that people could be really hypocritical and they would tell you something nice in the face, while they mock you behind your back. You listen to your friend with understanding for some time, your attention being pointed at how you can't trust people even if they appear to be nice when they talk to you. Later on, you stop at a store to buy a bottle of water and the lady behind the counter looks at you and says: "Your hair is so... nice!"

You mumble a "thank you," give her a mean look to show her that you understand what she was really getting at and storm out of the store. You are wondering how people could be so hypocritical and tell you something nice when they don't really mean it. The lady watches you walk out of the door, wondering how come a person could be so rude after being complimented. You've just experienced being primed by the conversation with your friend and reacted based on the priming without even knowing it.

In the moment of making a decision, most of the times, the choice is made on an unconscious level without our conscious participation. If comparison or further analysis is required, your conscious attention is called for a second opinion, but the available choices would already be filtered and reduced to a minimum by the prior mind-programming, the current mood, and priming.

A decision is nothing more than a cause and effect process where your conscious choices are very limited, in most cases reduced to only one. There's nothing wrong with this. You are not a bad person.

You may have heard of the importance to forgive yourself for past mistakes. The importance of forgiving yourself is to relieve the burden of guilt from your shoulders, so that you can focus your energy on more constructive projects. Guilt does not pre-pave success. Remember when we talked about our ancestors that lived in caves and the two important things they had to take care of was to eat and not get eaten? In modern times, guilt is our wild beast that eats us. Guilt is worse for your emotional and physical health than probably any junk food that you can think of. It may seem morally right to feel guilty about something in your past, but feeling guilty is a futile effort with no benefits, as you have no control over the past. You need to forgive yourself.

In fact, you can go as far as saying that you don't even need to forgive yourself. You've done nothing wrong in the first place. It was a cause and effect principle in action that defined your choices. You are not bad because of it. Your choice is only what it is: an effect after a cause. Don't wait for somebody or something from outside to give you permission to relieve the guilt. If you hold on to guilt, you are programming your mind to judge you as not good enough and in turn, you limit your vision for future choices. There are no mistakes. There are only learning experiences and valuable data that can help us in the future.

The way to make your future choices better is to build a more clear-minded and success-oriented mind environment. Part of building such an environment is releasing the guilt as soon as possible. By releasing the guilt, you are pre-paving your better decisions long before you are faced with a choice.

View mistakes as a good thing! Mistakes often hold important life lessons. Like anything else, it is neither good, nor bad. It takes the role you assign it. You are the Manager. Why make it a brick that you carry, when you can make it a brick that you can step on.

"Success in life is the result of good judgment. Good judgment is usually the result of experience. Experience is usually the result of bad judgment."

Anthony Robbins

How Guilt Affects Your Mind Environment

The feeling of guilt is one of the most detrimental mind immobilizers. It makes you point your attention to yourself in a very negative way. In the moments of guilt, you perceive yourself as bad, inappropriate and incapable of being a "good" person. Because of it, you start developing an attitude that you are not deserving of good things happening to you. This programs your mind into thinking that when you have desires, you are not worthy of having them, since you've done so poorly in being what you are expected to be. This programming filters your choices when the time for a decision comes. It keeps you in a stressed state, a state of fight-or-flight. You start to view your environment as hostile. You have become your own enemy.

Moral Values

The purpose of the whole guilt system in our society is to ensure conformity with the group's agreement of what is acceptable behavior in society. But this rigid moral system is not very well defined. Even in your own family, the expectations of what is wrong or right change constantly. What you were taught is right by one person may not be what is right for somebody else. Additionally, as times change, the moral values change as well. Some people live by the older rules, while others upgraded their list. Which ones do you comply with, then?

As I've mentioned, I grew up in communism. They did a very thorough job of instilling a carefully selected moral value set to ensure the longevity of the communist system. Not much information could penetrate the iron wall. Only certain books were allowed and you would get in all sorts of trouble if you got caught reading the wrong literature with "bad" influence. Music was limited, information was limited, and there was a constant flow of propaganda in our school system to ensure that we grew up to be good communists.

I was 14 when the system crashed. One morning, we woke up and it was done. Just like that. And just like that, I was left wondering, now what? How do I know what is right anymore, now that everything we were taught before was renounced? In the framework of guilt, I needed to know from now on, please tell me, what should I feel guilty about doing or not doing, so I can have the most updated version of the moral list? For months we didn't know how to handle this new freedom. As teenagers, we expressed it in going to school in our pajamas, or coloring our hair in many different colors. Anything to experience what it felt like not to have to conform.

I've always been very grateful for that experience. It showed me at an early age to be alert to what are considered established social norms. Social moral systems are transient and as such, cannot be trusted as universal truths. Two hundred years ago, if you got pregnant and had a baby without being married, society would turn against you and denounce you for what you did. Today, for the very same act, society would kindly help you with financial and moral support. Would our scared unmarried pregnant great, great grandmothers have even thought that their "shameful" act would be a perfectly normal thing sometime in the future? Instead, they were proclaimed to be adulteresses and forced to carry the burden of guilt for what they've done to themselves, to society and to their child.

Just as we've learned that worry or stress is not necessarily a bad thing, installed moral principles in society are not to be viewed negatively either. It's about looking at scenarios from a viewpoint of cause and effect, rather than a judgment of good or bad. If you cultivate a powerful, higher state of mind, you won't have the need to consult the moral value system anyway. You will naturally be loving, compassionate and stable in your stands. In our essence, we are all love. It is our fears and insecurities that cause us to lash out and act angrily or harmfully. It is the activation of the fight-or-flight that causes anything from mild frustration to an aggressive, violent act. In its base, it is all fear. It's your limbic system - the emotional region of the brain - in action. And when things have escalated enough, fear overcomes the power of reason and engages your prefrontal cortex to justify the anger and create new, better ways to fight. As you clean up your mind immobilizers, your fears and insecurities will subside and your true self will start shining. People and circumstances won't be annoying. You will be able to look at them with appreciation and often admiration. You will be happier, freer and in a state of gratitude. Things around you will amaze you the way they did when you were a child. You can be a beacon of light and inspiration for others. You can shine your love on them and they will like it because when they see themselves through your eyes, they will see their worth and this will empower them. You won't have to worry if you are doing the right thing anymore because you will know your own worth, as well as the worth of those around you. Your actions will be filtered through this powerful mindset. You won't have to make others feel guilty for what happens to you because you will know that you are the creator of your reality and you will understand that they also have their own voices in their head that called them to whatever action they took. [13]

Guilt as Manipulation

Guilt as manipulation is so widely used that even though we may know that we are being manipulated at the time, we want to avoid the guilt so much that we comply with what is requested from us anyway. I put it to good use with my mom when I was growing up. It brought me a lot of goodies back then, but in the long run, it created bad habits that I had to work on changing.

It goes like this. Somebody sends a message that what we did or didn't do was bad. You, in turn, start feeling guilty about your behavior. After all, this is what is expected of you if you care. The next step would be for you to act on that guilt and make efforts to remedy the situation, which means compliance with their request for a specific behavior. Congratulations - you were just manipulated by guilt!

This manipulation game started when you were very young and your parents wanted to make sure that you grow up to be a good person. You may have heard things like:

"I work hard to provide for you and this is how you respond?"

"You should be ashamed of yourself!"

"You're giving me grey hair!"

In the majority of cases, these are situational comments with no real bad intent behind them. Regardless, those comments made you an active participant in the guilt game. Guilt manipulation continued with friends and teachers. You became part of a self-regulating system that used guilt to keep you in line with an agreed upon socially acceptable framework. Later on, in adulthood, this pattern continued to evolve and repeat itself over and over in various relationships.

The guilt pattern is often played between spouses to ensure that the loved one doesn't deviate from the expected behavior. It is expressed in hurtful looks, words, silence, or a halt in the participation of the three Fs - Food, Fun and ... well, you can guess. All done to notify you that the line of allowed behavior has been crossed and that you should feel guilty.

Friends have their demands as well. When they ask for something, you often have to put your own interests in the backburner, so that you can be the good and selfless friend that you are supposed to be. "I'm the most selfless person I know, so you should put ME first!" Says your "selfless" friend. Whatever the demand is, the feeling of guilt puts you in a position to question your own judgment, lose confidence in your decisions and let others guide your choices. Gradually, you forget how to use your own inner compass because you let others select the direction of your actions from fear of feeling guilty later on. Your mind, instead of being strong and knowing your worth, becomes weak and in need of approval from outside.

Creating Ripples Guilt

Creating Ripples type of guilt makes us feel bad for causing damage into somebody else's life. When you take responsibility for other people's unhappiness, you start acting in ways that will ensure that your behavior doesn't make them upset. Better safe than sorry, better act in ways that keep them happy than get them upset and then feel guilty about it. The fear of creating ripples in other people's lives can create ripples in many other areas in your own life. Instead of being a human being that freely expresses your emotions and works to realize your own potential, you become a human being that expresses your emotions only in ways that won't potentially affect others negatively. You become a human being that is trying to fix other people's problems to reduce the number of unhappy people around you and thus reduce your load of responsibility a little.

There are things in life that we incorrectly take responsibility for. You can't be responsible for other people's choices. That's an inside job through and through! You can't feel guilty enough to fix somebody else's life.

When you release the responsibility for other people's choices of how they feel, you can start gaining your power. From a powerful standpoint, the ripples that you create are ripples that make others stronger. Not by modifying your behavior to keep them happy, but by living by example and by being a stable person that your friends can go to for support. A lighthouse doesn't run around telling ships there is a shore nearby. It just stands there, shining its light for when ships need it. That's how it's the most helpful.

Also, just like you, others are the creators, the Managers of their own lives. If what you did caused "damage" in their life, it is because that's what their mind environment was set for. It's what they were allowing at the time. You were a participant in their story that they created. Just like you attract and manifest experiences that match your mindset, so others are doing the same. And just like others show up and play by the tone you've set for your life, so did you in their story.

Self-Damage Guilt

The self-damage guilt cycle goes like this: you come up with a resolution, like start a diet tomorrow. When tomorrow comes, your stomach looks at its clock: breakfast time! You can't fool it with the tiny piece of toast. Where's the rest? While your stomach is yelling for you to pay attention to it, your mind is going through the 6 grieving steps over losing the nice, crispy bacon strips with eggs. You realize that this is only the beginning of a long, hungry journey! This sample of what you're going to have to suffer all day has nothing on the sweet sound of sizzling bacon in the frying pan. You think, eh, I'll only have two strips today. But as soon as you do it, the smell of bacon sends you right to heaven. All thoughts about dieting have left the building. The next thing you remember is seeing the already empty plate in front of you with traces of egg yolk on its bottom. Your stomach is filled with eggs and bacon and your mind is now filled with guilt. The better the food tasted, the worse the guilt. You got rid of the hunger monster, but now you have another monster to deal with - guilt. Is this a no-win situation?

Okay, you think. A new resolution is created that starts first thing tomorrow morning. A strict diet is in place that will make up for all the deviations from the previous resolution. Well, chances are, the bacon will win tomorrow as well. And the next day. And the next day. Each day, the bacon overpowers you, the guilt monster rears its ugly head.

Why do we engage in self-sabotaging behavior and keep playing this stepping forward and backward Tango dance? Isn't it only logical to make a decision, stick with it and enjoy the successful outcome that we envisioned? Well, it is not that easy. A successful diet is quite literally, mind over platter.

When talking about a change in your behavior, what makes the difference between success and failure is the strength of your willpower. A will without power is a dead giveaway. Similar to a muscle, if the willpower is strong, the change requires less effort and you are soon on your way to a better you. If your willpower is weak, the journey is strenuous and we often give up, postponing it for another moment in time, usually tomorrow. Not because we think we would be stronger tomorrow, but because we are too weak to handle the effort that is required of us now.

What are the things that weaken your willpower? Among other things, the guilt you felt after your failure. Guilt takes a large amount of energy from you and diminishes your willpower. It is a mind immobilizer that puts you into cognitive dissonance and healing mode.

An interesting survey conducted by Professor Karen Pine from the University of Hertfordshire shows remarkable results about the absurdity in our behavior when we are under stress. 79% of the women in the survey said that they would go on a shopping spree to cheer themselves up. According to Professor Pine, some women use shopping as an emotion regulator to make them feel better when they were feeling down. The paradox is that worrying about money could lead women to spend more! Worrying about your weight can make you eat more. Worrying about not working out can glue you to the couch.[14]

When we are under stress, we are compelled to look for a quick way out. We are under the influence of cognitive dissonance. Our brain is on a rescue mission: it is calling our immediate attention to something that will make us feel better quickly. It switches to immediate reward seeking mode. As a result, you start craving whatever food, substance or activity your brain associates with the promise of reward. Your brain convinces you that this reward is the only way to feel better. While in a normal, non-stressed state you would weigh the pros and the cons and most probably you would avoid the reward, in a stressed state you will only think about the good feelings you think you'll get, leaving the downsides to shrink into the distance.

Can you see how guilt takes you right back into the cycle that you are trying to get out of? Guilt is a very strong stressor. It is a Catch 22 situation. When you feel guilty about failing, the guilt makes your mind weaker and to compensate for it, it guides you back into the behavior you are trying to avoid, which in turn brings you back to failure.

When you fail in anything, it is not the failure itself that triggers the stress. It is the feelings of shame, guilt, loss of control, and loss of hope that make failures seem like the end of the world. This leads to a weaker mind and more failures. Before you know it, you've programmed your mind to expect disappointments and re-occurring cycles of guilt.

Guilt won't motivate you to positive results. Sometimes, the discomfort of guilt may increase the power of the desire enough for you to take action. But if you don't have long-term resolution for your guilt and change your patterns of thought regarding it, the heavy load of stress it carries will eventually take you back to weaker states of mind.

When you have setbacks that you may perceive as failures, don't be hard on yourself. Let go of the guilt as soon as you notice its presence.

The study was prepared by two psychologists - Claire Adams at Louisiana State University and Mark Leary at Duke University. They invited young, healthy, weight-watching women who were told that the study would first evaluate the reactions to eating experiences while watching television, and then afterward, perform a taste test for several types of candies. The purpose of the experiment was to evaluate how guilt and self-forgiveness affected women's ability for self-control. Upon their arrival, the participants were asked to drink a full glass of water "to clear the palette." The real purpose of the drink was to give them a feeling of fullness. Next, the women were asked to select one of two doughnuts (original and chocolate flavor) while watching a video. When they were done, they filled out the questionnaire and were instructed to wait for the second study. Before the second study began, the researcher gave half the women a specially designed message. The researcher explained that sometimes people eat unhealthy, sweet foods while watching TV and that was the reason for the experimenters' choice of doughnuts. The researcher also explained that the women may feel guilty for eating the doughnut but it was okay, there was no reason to feel really bad about it. It was only a little doughnut anyway and everyone eats unhealthily sometimes. The other women were not given any message at all.

In the second part of the study, all women were served three large bowls of candy. Each bowl was weighed beforehand. The participants were given a rating sheet to evaluate the candy for taste, texture, and goodness. Before the researcher left the room, the women were instructed that they had to taste at least one of each type of candy, but they were welcome to help themselves to as much as the liked. So who do you think ate more? The women told not to feel guilty or the women given no message at all?

Logically, the women that were still feeling guilty about the doughnut should have eaten less. The women who were told that it's okay to eat unhealthy sometimes should eat more, taking the message as permission to self-indulge. In fact, the opposite happened. The participants who were relieved of the guilt ate 28 grams of candy, while the ones that were not encouraged to forgive themselves ate almost 70 grams - nearly three times as much. [15]

So, if tomorrow you don't follow your resolution for the day, just accept it without any judgment and let go of the guilt as soon as you sense it gripping you. It's fine to acknowledge the guilt, but don't let yourself wallow or be consumed by it. Have you seen those little dogs that bark like crazy and pretend to be scary? Guilt is like a little barking dog. If you are afraid of it and you are trying to run away or chase it away, it will keep barking because your reaction to it makes the barking fun. If you stop paying attention to it and move on to something more constructive, eventually it will get bored and will leave you alone. There is no reason for you to feel bad about something that you can't change. But there is a high cost you would be paying if you do: a weakened mind.

Guilt is Poisonous

When you feel guilty, the underlying message that you are feeding to your mind is that you are not good enough. When you or others make you feel guilty for your actions, you start questioning your judgment. You doubt your self-worth and look outward for validation. Even though you have everything you need to be an empowered person, you've been trapped by the guilt cycle.

No matter what the type of the guilt is in your life, I would urge you to take inventory of the backpack of rocks that you are carrying and understand how that backpack is absolutely unnecessary. The amazing thing about choosing to live without guilt is that you will start basing your decisions on your own judgment. If others use manipulation through guilt to request a specific behavior, if you don't participate in the guilt game, they will soon learn that it doesn't work with you and will leave you alone. There is absolutely no benefit for you to carry guilt. Guilt is inhibiting the successful and powerful mindset that you are capable of having and has zero benefits. Train yourself out of the habit of feeling guilty. There are no mistakes. It is all a cause-and-effect process. Understand it and only get involved in what benefits you. This won't make you selfish. It will empower you and as an empowered human being, you can be of much more help to others than from a confused and insecure place of mind. Feed a powerful mind environment, not a powerful guilt system. Keep referring back to your emotions as your MIMS and keep growing.

How to Resolve Guilt

If you are carrying guilt, don't feel guilty for feeling guilty. Accept that the past is the past and that you had guilt at that time. Now it's time to re-frame your guilt.

If you feel guilty about having caused damage in somebody else's life, do your best to reach resolution as fast as you can. If you have to, apologize and own up to your actions. If you can make it right, make it right. Don't try to cover it - just do whatever it takes to resolve it. We will take on the topic of blame later in this book. Don't worry about this now. Focus on freeing yourself of guilt.

When you recognize guilt getting a grip on you, talk yourself out of it by understanding that the best way to make things better is to release the guilt quickly. You can't change the past, no matter how guilty you feel. Accept the fact that others around you may like or dislike some of your choices. No matter what you do, you will always be faced by disapproval from someone. Learn to approve of yourself, not look for others to approve of you. When approval from others is not priority, the guilt for the disapproval will gradually disappear. Also, think about your value system. How many values do you have that sincerely matter to you, and how many have been pushed onto you by society?

Teach the people around you that you will no longer participate in their attempts to manipulate you. This may require you to face some disapproval and disappointment. You can communicate your stands clearly and without fear of being disapproved of. People learn quickly - when they see that guilt doesn't work, they will soon stop wasting their efforts.

Don't feel guilty about tending to your own needs. That's actually your main responsibility. You can be best for others when you are at your best. Try to do more "selfish" things that would normally make you feel guilty that you put yourself first.

If you are not perfect in your life, you are not alone. The rest of the Earth's population isn't either. If you didn't do what you had planned to do or broke your diet, release the guilt right away and do your best to stick with your plans. Guilt will not motivate you in long run. It will take away your willpower. Guilt is a mind immobilizer that creates a habit of thought that you are not deserving of good things. This is absolutely false. You deserve to be empowered. You deserve good things in your life.

Not Knowing Your Worth

Your Worth through the Eyes of Others

Have you heard that beauty is in the eyes of the beholder? I can tell you that no matter how much I thought my nose needed an immediate plastic surgery when I was a teenager, my mom found it the most beautiful nose she had ever seen. Mom, are you looking at the same nose that I see in the mirror?

I know a few really good photographers. What makes them good is that they are able to see what is invisible to others - the beauty in the ordinary life. An older person may not find their wrinkled face beautiful, but when a photographer with an eye for beauty takes a snapshot, that same wrinkled skin becomes a magical representation of all the joys and hardships in life.

When we look at something, we don't just see it for what it is. We associate it with a prior experience that defines our current view. We distort the image through our own perception. When you look at somebody, you may find them annoying, amusing, pleasant, funny, scary, intimidating, or anything that your associations with prior experience allow you to see. Your mood also plays a role. If you feel weaker at that moment and want peace and quiet, a loud, self-confident person may be too much to handle and you may unconsciously feel uncomfortable in their presence. You change depending on your mood and prior experience.

This brings us to how you define your self-image. If you are like most people, you have been gathering feedback from others for as long as you remember and applying it to your grade of self-worth. When you were little and still learning to navigate in this new to you world, your mom was your guidance for what is safe and what could be potentially dangerous. With every new thing that you ventured, you checked to see if mom approved. She was like a barometer for you to help you learn to safely move around. Later on, you found the importance of having your teachers' approval. The more likeable you were, the easier it was to gain approval. But what about those people who didn't like you? What about the ones that criticized you? What about the ones that made you feel unworthy? You gathered that data and took points off from your self-worth score. What about the times you acted naturally and others found it inappropriate? Points off. What happened when you saw all those images in the magazines of perfect skin and body that you didn't have? Points off.

Have you ever been to a house of mirrors? They distort your image into something very funny. One could make your head huge and your body small. Another could make your legs triple in size. They are all distortions of the real you.

People are like curved mirrors. When they look at you, they see an image that is distorted through their own insecurities, troubles, personal experiences and mood. What they reflect back at you is that distorted image which is not you, but their distortion of you. Some people like you. Others disapprove of you. None of it has anything to do with you.

In a way, society has established very high standards for us, normal people, to feel good. You wish you could look like a model. Well, take a picture of yourself now and you can look just like them 3 months later. Because that's how long it would take you to learn basic Photoshop! It's not real. C'mon, we all have runny noses sometimes, we all fart and we all get baggy eyes if we don't get enough sleep.

Society also teaches us to let others recognize our strengths. You can't just say that you are smart: this is for the others to determine and pronounce. You can't say that you are good at something: the rating of your goodness will be duly noted in the evaluation that you get from others. We learn to judge our worth by the approval from outside.

The system of basing your worth on things that are outside of your body and control is sketchy, especially if the people assessing your worth want you to be a Hollywood model, or a mother of two behind a white picket fence. Plus, we have no control over what others think of us.

Basing your self-worth on how much you've accomplished from your list of goals is another futile effort. No matter how much you accomplish, there will always be more to achieve. Also, some goals naturally take a little longer. Would you pronounce yourself unworthy just because you are mid-journey to your new desire for success and give up? Would you go on a road trip to another city and start feeling discouraged somewhere in the middle because you are not there yet?

Instead of looking outside for proof and confirmation that you are worthy, you have to look inside. There is a powerful being there, with enormous potential for anything that you may want to create. There is a powerful being longing to express itself and grow. There is a being that is perfect in every way, knowing how to love and appreciate life. There is a being that wants to live joyfully and savor the moments with all the different tastes life has to offer. Your worth is a given. You don't need to prove it. You don't need to look for things outside of you to confirm it. It's there, 100% organic and worthy. Guaranteed!

What happens when you let outside circumstances define you? Instead of looking at yourself directly, you look at your reflection in the distorted mirrors of others. This leads you to believe that you don't have enough to be loveable, likeable, accepted, or to live a fulfilled life. You stop trusting yourself. You lose your self-confidence.

"He who trims himself to suit everyone will soon whittle himself away."

Raymond Hull

Selfishness and Selflessness

We are taught that we should put the wellbeing of others above our own. I have a friend who started going to yoga classes after work. Even though she needed the classes for her back, she felt very guilty that she was selfishly spending time for herself, instead of being home for her family.

For a long time I thought that choosing to take care of myself, instead of being there for others, was a bad thing to do. The exact opposite is true. How do unhappy people try to achieve your attention? By yelling, guilt trips, blaming, demanding you to change, demanding you to give them what they want, harassing you, or trying to control you. If they had taken care of their own emotional stability first, they would be strong people that knew how to handle their lives without demanding your immediate compliance with their requirements. Their happiness would make your life better, even if that happiness stemmed from the fact that they merely weren't yelling at you all the time anymore. Your personal happiness is the best gift you could give to others.

Think about being on an airplane. When you listen to the safety instructions, the Flight Attendant tells you that in an emergency, before you try to help somebody else with their oxygen mask, make sure you put on yours first!

Unless you can take care of yourself, you can't give much to others. When you've neglected your wellbeing and you live in self-doubt, you start trying to compensate for it in a variety of ways. Why do people get jealous, for example, and act out on their jealousy in unpleasant ways? They don't trust that they are good enough to be able to keep their loved ones, so they try to establish security by limitations and control. Why do people get mad at us for our choices? These are their insecurities talking, trying to compensate what they perceive they are lacking. Why do people choose to get offended by something that we said? Because they feel unstable in their knowledge that they are a complete and perfect human being regardless of anything from the outside. The message that they are giving us is: "Please, show me that I matter to you because I feel very unimportant and I need to make up for it by being important to you."

If you are looking for validation of your self-worth in other people and you don't receive it, your insecurities start bending your perception of others. You may see them as cold, cruel, or insensitive. You may start finding faults to justify that the reason they acted the way they did is not because of you, but because they are not good people in general. They, in turn, see their distorted reflection of them in your responses and this can cause their own insecurities to kick in. Everyone participates in this distortion. That's how we've been taught.

Don't Let Others Change You

We've all had experiences when we made a joke that was misinterpreted. The person felt unimportant, or offended by what you said or did. The message is conveyed to you right away. When someone throws a fit about your behavior, you learn fast - you don't want to have them throw the fit again, so you have two choices: you keep doing what you are doing and deal with their fits. Or you modify your behavior around them to avoid the fit from happening again. But before jumping on one of the choices, you need to understand that their interpretation of what you did or didn't do is outside of your control and often it has very little to do with you. If you start accommodating their requests and act according to their requirements to avoid them getting upset again, you enter a game that is not beneficial for either you or them. First of all, you teach them that throwing a fit around you works, so the quick learners that they are, they naturally start having expectations that whenever they want you to modify your choices, you are going to listen and perform accordingly.

Secondly, you are training yourself to put others' voices as more valid than your own in determining the direction of your decisions. The more you do it, the more you encourage such behavior from others and the more that happens, the more you train yourself into thinking that you are the inappropriate one that needs the approval from outside. It is a lose-lose situation, but it doesn't have to be this way.

When I first brought my wonderful cat home, she used to get up early in the morning, wondering what fun things she could do next. In her kitty head, fun things often required getting my attention. For that reason, she had to get me out of bed. Cats are very skilled in doing that. It starts with a gentle purr next to your ear. Then, if that doesn't work, you may start feeling cat whiskers tickling you all over the face. If this doesn't work, a steady walk back and forth over your head is initiated. This is followed by meowing or more aggressive methods like walking all over your body and jumping on the bed in ways that pull you from sleep. Lastly, my cat would start running back and forth in the room, making as much noise as possible.

My cat performed that routine for a few weeks. She was determined to train the human into getting up and providing the requested attention. I knew that I had to make everything possible to train her out of that habit unless I wanted to be doomed to be out of bed by 5:30 a.m. regardless of how late I stayed up the night before. So, instead of showing any signs of reaction to her attempts, I completely ignored them and stubbornly remained in bed until I was ready to get up. It wasn't that easy not to move when cat paws were marching on my head and a cute little nose was pushing into my face. Eventually, she learned that the efforts of getting me out of bed when I was not ready were not producing results, so there was no more point in continuing to try. This was years ago. To this day, she stays in bed with me until I am ready wake, no matter what time I choose. This has made our relationship even better in the way that she is no longer expecting me to react to her attempts to get attention and I never stop to appreciate the fact that I have a cat that honors my sleep. It is a win-win situation.

You don't need to let others distract you from who you are or what is important to you. Nobody needs to understand your journey because it is exclusively yours to have. When you act from a place of stability in your ideas, actions, and stands, people soon learn, just like my cat did, that walking all over you in attempts to make you different does not produce any results, so they must eventually accept you as you are, or walk out of your life. In either case, it is a win-win for both sides.

"A 'No' uttered from deepest conviction is better and greater than a 'Yes' merely uttered to please, or, what is worse, to avoid trouble."

Mahatma Gandhi

Are You Ready for the Ride?

Now, let's look at knowing your self-worth from yet another perspective. Imagine riding a bike. And, imagine that maybe you haven't had a lot of practice, so you're not very confident or stable. Bumps on the road scare you because you are afraid you may fall. If it rains, the road gets wet and slippery, which you may see as dangerous. You only ride on paved roads because they are the smoothest. You only ride with others and follow their directions. You are cautious all the time. You are afraid. If others get in your way, you'll lose your balance. If they call for your attention, you get distracted and you fall. In fact, because you are not good at balancing, falling is constant and painful threat in your bike-riding experience. This only adds to your fears and lack of confidence.

Let's imagine the opposite. You are stable in your balance. You enjoy the ride. When you are on your bike, you have a sense of freedom and joy. You explore. You deviate from the paved roads because it is so much more fun to try new things. It feels like flying. You know what you are doing. Bumps - you love them because they only make the ride more exciting!

The same principles of bike riding apply to your self-worth. If you are unstable, your experience is diminished and your confidence low. You select security, even if it is not rewarding, because this is the only thing you can handle. The journey is not that much fun.

When you know your self-worth, life is a fun ride. Circumstances don't cause you to lose balance but motivate you and inspire you. Other people's voices don't dictate your life. No outside distraction can derail you. When you are stable in knowing your worth you define the course of events that happen to you and you decide how they affect your being.

Maybe you've heard people say that you are not the center of the Universe. Well I'm here to tell you that you are. You are the center of *your* Universe. Your worth is a given. You are a powerful human being with unlimited potential. You have the gift of focused attention that can take you in any direction that you choose. You can create any reality for yourself that you please. You have the full capacity to live and enjoy life to the fullest. You know who you are and you don't let others or past experiences define you. You don't have to wait a day longer to start your gradual path of learning your true self and loving it. Believe me, there is a lot to love there. Loving others starts with loving yourself.

"Love is the bridge between you and everything."

Rumi

A Whole New Meaning of Loving Yourself

You've probably heard people say that it is important to love yourself. How do you go about loving yourself?

Expressing the love for yourself happens by accepting and loving your life. You love yourself when you are in peace with your situation now, no matter what it is. You love yourself when you know your inherent and absolute self-worth. You love yourself when you are not afraid to be who you are for fear that others may not like it. You love yourself when you stand proud of what you've done and you look at the future, knowing that there is nothing impossible to you. You love yourself when your mind resides in higher states, free from the Mind Immobilizers.

A few years ago I started having back pain. I went to the doctor and it turned out that one of my legs is a little shorter, causing my spine to curve. I called my mom to tell her and this is what she said:

"When I gave birth to you, I checked for defects: I counted your toes, I counted your fingers and all was good. Don't blame me for giving you a shorter leg!"

Okay, I get it. I am out of warranty. My shorter leg is something I have to deal with. Do you think I'm sad about my shorter leg? Yes, I have to do exercises to make sure my back doesn't curve more, but this wonderful leg of mine is serving me well, taking me on adventurous hikes, making dancing possible; it looks good in a high heel shoe and I can still pick objects up with my toes. I have fully accepted the fact that it is shorter and it does not bother me a bit.

There is nothing I can do to make it longer. I can either choose to live happily or live miserably with a shorter leg. The leg itself isn't going to change.

Loving yourself is appreciating life and focusing on all the wonderful things it has to offer, rather than the things that we may find "defective." It's living your life to the fullest, expressing your potential with no fear.

Unconditional love is being aware of your worth, regardless of the conditions. Others around you don't have to be the way you want them to be in order for you to be happy. Circumstances don't have to be perfect. You don't have to be perfect. When you don't require conditions to change before you can be happy and stable, you are enjoying unconditional love. You don't need anything from outside to prove that you are worthy. The fact is that you are unconditionally worthy. And that's a given.

How to Remember Your Self Worth

You are absolutely self-worthy and you've always been. All you need to do is find a way of remembering and knowing it again. When you were little, you didn't question your self-worth. You were busy enjoying life as much as you could. You didn't question your self-worth because you didn't yet know you could be deemed unworthy. That came later, as you trained yourself to believe that you were not good enough.

To start remembering your self-worth and start loving yourself again, you need to fully accept yourself and your life as they are. Don't confuse your self-worth with your behavior, your accomplishments or the response you get from others. There will never be a point in your life when all opinions about you are perfect and everything in your life is perfect. First, you can't control what others think of you.

Secondly, your life will never be perfect because you continue to generate new desires that make your life less-than perfect until you reach them. You can never stop having new desires. Yet, you are as perfect as you can be in any moment in time.

Your innate perfection has nothing to do with perfectionism. Perfectionism isn't about doing your best or about reaching your highest potential. Perfectionism is an attempt to avoid being judged and blamed by yourself or others. It is about gaining approval and acceptance. If you fully accept yourself with all your imperfections, you can allow your authentic, true self to shine through more and more. When you suppress your true self for fear of disapproval, you lose your own inner compass and you become shaped by others, rather than the true you inside. This translates to you as anxiety, depression, confusion, resentment and blame. It robs you of the dreams you don't go for because you are afraid that you will fail, disappoint others, or make mistakes.

To learn again to accept yourself and accept your absolute worth is one of the hardest battles. It takes a lot of courage to step against the current of social norms and ideas about what you should be. Having to fit in is an engrained need in us, going back to ancient times, when being part of the group meant survival. It takes decision and practice. Yet, if you look around, people who are liked the most are those that can be authentically themselves, honest, true to their inner being and down to earth.

Accepting yourself also takes letting go of comparing yourself to others. We tend to take score in our social group who is ahead and who is falling behind. You are unique, just like everybody else. It is your uniqueness that holds your greatest strengths, talents and potential. You are completely original and cannot be compared.

Gratitude

One of the fastest ways to reconnect with your self-worth is practicing gratitude. It's easy to cultivate and it's incredibly powerful. It is also one of the most beneficial nutrients for a good mind environment. It gradually changes your habits to put your attention to what you want and what you appreciate.

Recently, I went on a trip to the Dominican Republic. I was taking a lot of pictures that I put in two separate albums. One was called "Ugly Reality," the other one, "Incredible Beauty." In the "Ugly Reality," I put pictures of trash in the sea, live electrical cables hanging on the streets, chaotic traffic and overwhelming poverty. In the other album, I had pictures of unbelievable natural beauty, turquoise-water and white-sand beaches, colorful exotic fruit, smiling people, people dancing and singing, Caribbean style décor, kindness on the faces of ordinary people, expressions of art, beautiful families together. When I look at the "Ugly Reality" photos, I can sense how I lose my power. I feel that it is unfair to have such conditions in our modern age. When I look at the "Incredible Beauty" album, I am filled with gratitude. I look at the abundant natural beauty and I am humbled and touched by it. When I look at this album, I can feel my heart filling up to the brim with appreciation and admiration.

Your attention is like that camera I used in the Dominican Republic. You can point it to any reality that you choose. You can zoom in on all the imperfections in your life. Or, you can zoom out and see it in a little larger perspective - there are a lot of things that you haven't done yet, but so many that you've accomplished. Finally, you can point your attention to what makes you grateful. It may be a person that you love and admire, art, natural beauty, birds outside, technology, a good movie, or anything that awakens in you a sense of gratitude and admiration.

The attention snapshots that you take tell a story. It could be a story of an unhappy world, or a story of a beautiful world. As the purpose of this exercise is to reconnect with your self-worth, I would suggest that you create in your mind or on your computer a "Gratitude" album. Go on a hunt for wonderful moments and expressions and place them in the album. You can store them as a memory in your head, an item in a list, or a picture in a photo album. Every day, look for something to feel grateful for. Try to stay focused on it for a while, allowing it to touch you as fully as possible. Close your eyes, smile, and give your thanks.

By practicing gratitude, you are dramatically changing your mind environment. First of all, stress and gratitude are self-excluding. This means that when you are in gratitude, you are not activating the fight-or-flight response. There is no fear. The more moments in your day you devote to being grateful, the more you are training yourself out of the fear-based habits like blame, guilt and worry. As a result, your mind is getting stronger and stronger.

Something else starts happening too. You are building a new habit of focusing on what is good around you. It naturally spills over many different areas, including your own life and self. You start appreciating your uniqueness, the powerful being inside, the wonderful things you've done. Your focus changes from what doesn't work in your life to what does work in your life. Even if you are unable to see yourself for the wonderful person you really are at this moment in time, after practicing gratitude, your self-worth will come naturally. Gratitude also changes your general mind environment. Instead of focusing on what you don't want, you are now actively practicing habits of focusing on what you want in general. This immediately puts your attitude in a more positive setting.

Not knowing your worth is a mind immobilizer that creates a habit of thought that makes you seek outside validation and ignore your own inner voice.

Blame

After reading about how your social environment has trained you into different patterns of thoughts that are not beneficial to you, you may start thinking that all the "bad" things that ever happened to you are their fault. You've been a victim of social conditioning. Before you go any further, stop! You are entering another danger zone that could hinder your manifesting experience - blame.

Blame may feel a lot better than guilt because this time, you are the innocent one. Now you can point your finger at them and shake your head. But when you blame others for what has happened to you, the underlying messages are:

1.)   I am not responsible for what happened to me.

2.)   I am a victim who has been mistreated by fate or by others.

You may be right to be upset if somebody mistreated you, misled you, took advantage of you, or hurt you in any way. The fact that you are right in being upset, however, does not justify you in holding onto the blame. Not because they don't deserve it: Because you don't. You don't deserve to hold this poisonous feeling inside. There is nothing that you can do to change what happened by being upset. But there is a lot you can change in your future by releasing the blame and moving on.

A few years ago, a friend of mine, Kevin, went through a divorce. His ex wife ended up getting a large portion of his paycheck every month as alimony. Every time I would meet him at parties and gatherings, he looked like somebody had sucked the life out of him. He'd continuously talk about how mad he was, how she took his house, and now how she was getting his money every month. It wasn't fair, he kept saying. He was furious at the thought that she was having a great time with her new lover, living in his house, spending his money.

I remember Kevin before the divorce. He was a great guy to be around, always up to something, like building a greenhouse or fixing some new contraption on his boat. He had endless projects that his creative and fun-loving nature enjoyed. After the divorce, that all changed. He became angry at the whole world. It's like somebody replaced the Kevin that we knew. His mindset had changed; he had allowed blame to envelope his whole being. Because he felt like a victim from the divorce, that victim attitude was starting to show in different relationships at work and with friends. Kevin was blaming the world. He had developed a victim mentality.

Was he justified in his anger and blame? Absolutely. Did his ex wife deserve the blame? I don't know. What I did know is that Kevin didn't deserve it. He didn't deserve to live like that. He didn't deserve the monster that was eating him inside.

It took Kevin a while to step out of the self-torture machine of blame. He met a girl that he fell in love with. Shortly after that, he made the payments to his ex-wife automatic, so he wouldn't have to keep looking at the checks each month. Gradually, Kevin refocused his attention back to what was good in his life. He was gaining his strength back. It took him a few years to completely recover. With the help of his girlfriend, who is now his wife, he started his own business and now he is the owner of a very successful online marketing company. What he pays his ex is only a very small fraction of what he makes – too insignificant for him to worry about.

"It's funny," he says. "I hated my ex for taking my money away every month. But now I'm grateful for it because if it wasn't for the reduced money in my bank account, I wouldn't have gone out there to start my own business and make up for what I had lost. I have it all now: a loving wife and plenty of money in my bank."

Blame is not about if the other person deserves it or if you were in the right all the way. It's really about whether we deserve to poison our own well being with blame. You are a powerful person. You don't need to step into the shoes of a victim.

"To forgive is to set a prisoner free and discover that the prisoner was you."

Lewis Smedes

How Blame Affects Your Goals

When you blame, you put the responsibility for what happens to you in the hands of people or events outside. You take the role of the victim. Once you've taken that role, you enter a whole new story with three types of characters: victims, victimizers and occasional rescuers. Because you are looking at the world around you through the lens of a victim, you start filtering your experiences to support that mindset. You prime your mind to be sensitive to situations where others treat you badly or bad things happen to you. When the victim mentality is active, victimizers are very easy to find.

People who have chosen to play the victim game to the extreme can be difficult to handle. Because they feel powerless, they make good use of guilt trips and emotional blackmail to get their way. You may have met people who paradoxically seem to be addicted to the process of getting hurt and begging to be helped all at once. They attract problematic situations, failure, or mistreatment, even when it is clear to anyone else that there are better options right in front of them.

Victims feel that outside forces are bringing the bad things their way, so they are unable to focus on anything but the problem. Because of the victim attitude, even when victims call for people to help them, it is only to prove that the rescue attempts are going to be a failure. Drama is their way of finding relief.

We've all played the victim at some point. What is important to know is that playing this role keeps your attitude strongly focused into the problem. When the attitude is there, the solution can't come into being. Being a victim is a powerless state of mind. If you notice yourself playing the victim, stop immediately. Instead of blaming and feeling like a victim, you can look at the situation with real eyes. You can focus on the difficulties of this opportunity as a victim or you can see the difficulties as an opportunity for an empowered person. A problem ceases being a problem in the moment when you stop defending it and focus on a solution.

Kevin built a successful online business because his experience had created a money vacuum by putting him in a position where he felt his finances were in danger. When he released the blame and stopped the storm in his mind, the potential of his desire unfolded and made him the wealthy owner of a great company. When Kevin was eventually able to switch his efforts away from focusing on the problem, he was able to jump on the opportunity. The greatest success stories start with a hardship anyway. The ones that shake our world the most have the potential to be our greatest teachers for successes.

How to Release Blame

When somebody does something "bad" to you, it gives you the opportunity to generate a very strong desire for improvement in your life. This may be a completely new desire, or add more power to something that you had already wanted. In Kevin's case, before the divorce happened, he already had desires for a harmonious relationship and more financial abundance. The divorce put an end to the story of him and his ex wife. But it also started a new story that wonderfully supported his desires for a loving relationship and more money. It propelled Kevin to become the person he wanted to be.

Nothing that happens in your life is good or bad. It is what you define it to be. If you define the experience as bad for you, your life will keep proving that you're right. If you define it as a beginning of something better, your life will respond to your wishes in kind.

The Need to Control What You Can't

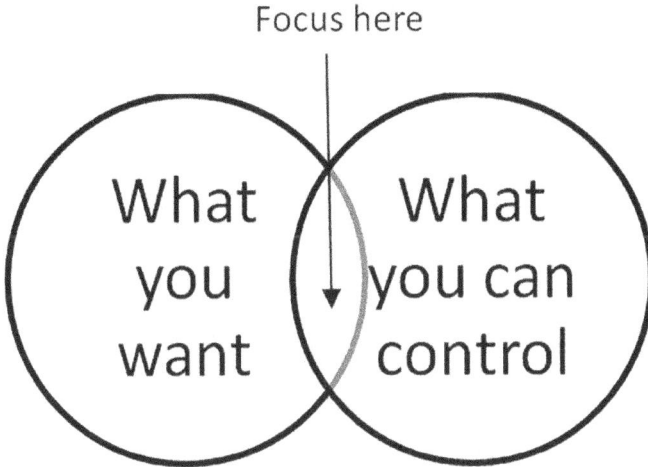

Focus here

What you want

What you can control

When I was seven, my parents sent me to swimming classes. I was a part of a group of fifteen kids. Out of the fifteen, fourteen of the kids successfully learned to swim. One kid just couldn't get it. That kid was me. Finally, the trainer told my mom that I should just quit. After begging my mom not to send me to another swim class, she acquiesced, and I didn't have to take another swimming lesson. It wasn't like I didn't like the water. I adored playing in the water, as long as I could feel the bottom under my feet.

When I was fifteen, a friend of mine got a free pass for one of the nicest pools in town and invited me to go with her. I knew I couldn't swim. But I also knew I could have fun, as long as I held onto a safety ring. She and I were going to meet at the hallway, so we could both use her pass to enter the pool area. I was excited!

The day I was supposed to meet my friend, I accidently left my swim cap behind, so I took a later bus to give myself enough time to backtrack and grab my swim cap. Little did I know, among the passengers on the late bus would be a boy who would light the bus on fire! Apparently, he lit a match and threw it under his bus seat, where a newspaper lay. We all had to exit the bus immediately.

Now, at this point, I'm pumping with adrenaline. The pool is only a block away, and I'm so eager to tell my friend what had just happened that I run the whole way there. Unfortunately, I was about 20 minutes late to our meeting spot, and she had already gone inside, leaving me with no pass, and no way to contact her (since this was before cell phones).

I was still pumping with energy. I waited until the check-in lady was looking away and snuck in. I rushed to the locker room and threw on my swimsuit. My heart rate could not calm down. It beat a hundred miles a minute. I was so worked up that the moment I got out into the pool, I saw my friend diving into the deep end, and without a second thought, I threw myself in after her!

It wasn't until I hit the cold water that I realized my mistake. I was in the deep end! There was no lifeguard, no place to hang on to. I couldn't swim! I flailed about, trying to kick like I was told to in class all those years ago, but to no avail. I was sinking; and sinking fast.

Was I going to die, just like that? It seemed so unreal. Then, out of nowhere, a thought occurred to me. I was wearing my rubber swim cap. I had backtracked home just to get it. In my panicked mind, I rationalized that rubber floats: I had seen rubber inner tubes. Rubber floats, and so I realized as long as I stopped moving and relaxed, the rubber cap would lift me up to the water's surface.

Of course the swim cap couldn't save me. But relaxing could. Without resistance, my body floated naturally, pushing my face back out into the air.

And from that moment on, I could swim.

I know now that the main reason I couldn't get the hang of swimming was because I was trying to force it. Swimming is something you learn naturally, not something that you try to control and force your body to learn. My body was already equipped to swim. I just needed the right circumstances to make me relinquish control. It was when I stopped struggling that I learned I could float.

People don't consciously walk. No one forces the arches to flex or to command a bend at the knee to be a certain angle. It just happens, without effort.

The problem with a lot of us is that we try to apply control where we can't, and not where we can. If you try to control the uncontrollable, you'll fail: your goals will remain unreached. This may make you conclude that you are not in charge of your life and nothing works the way you want it. This will become the lens through which you see the world.

In that pool, I had no control over my surroundings. I only had control over my mindset. Once my mindset had found its desire and pointed itself toward a wanted future (another day among the living), a natural manifestation of how that could happened occurred—In this case, the manifestation was the silly belief that my swim cap could make me float.

"I can't change the direction of the wind, but I can adjust my sails to always reach my destination."

Jimmy Dean

In your life, right now, you can only see what the circumstances currently represent. You have no way of seeing the full bigger picture. You don't always have enough knowledge to know the next step yet.

Even if a caterpillar has the knowledge that it will become a butterfly, it has no way of knowing what it is to be a butterfly because it doesn't have the experiential evidence of it. It can't imagine what it is to fly and see everything from a completely different point of view. In this same way, you don't know what your vantage point would be a few more steps down the road. But you can control the cultivation of trust that things are working steadily in your favor at all times, even when you don't see the next step yet. You can't control the economy of your country. You can't control the weather. Frankly, none of this is worth your time, anyway. What you have control over is your mental environment and your own personal growth into the person you would like to be. You can control your attitude toward life. And that's what makes the big difference. Your attitude is the success builder.

The Specific Details on Your Path

If you try to control the outcome of every specific detail and they don't turn out the way you wanted them to be, you may incorrectly conclude that you've reached a dead end or that you are generally not in control of your life. The thing is, a specific detail on your way is only a component of the bigger picture. Without having seen the bigger picture, you have no way of knowing the role of that specific component. Your conscious mind does not have the knowledge or capacity to evaluate it correctly yet. That component could create something wonderful, even if it's a huge blight in your life right now. That's why hindsight is always 20/20! You've already seen the bigger picture and you are able to clearly understand the component and its role.

Let me give you an example. When fledglings are born, their mother's nest provides a secure comfort zone for the little bird to grow strong. Whenever the fledging calls for it, food falls right into its beak. Then the comfort zone starts to change. Slowly, the mother will stand further and further away from the nest, forcing the baby bird to come out of the nest in order to get food. The first attempts often end with a fall on the ground, but, eventually, the little bird will learn that it can ease the falls by spreading its wings. This will motivate the baby bird to use its wings more and more. After a few weeks of practice, the little bird will learn more advanced techniques, like how to use the wind to lift, how to spot rising thermals and how to make controlled landings. In the process, birds develop the muscles necessary to flap their wings to their fullest potential.

A fledging does not try to control the circumstances. It does not get upset with the weather, or the behavior of their mom. It doesn't need a map of all the steps it has to take in order to fly. A baby bird doesn't get discouraged. It doesn't proclaim that the desire to fly is an impossible goal. It does not have the mind immobilizers that can get in the way, so its path to flying happens naturally. Over time, the birds build the muscles necessary in order to manifest the ability to successfully fly.

Well, congrats! You're that baby bird. You want to fly and you will. But there's an excellent chance that you'll take a few falls before you succeed. You can't control that; it's just part of learning to fly. But if you keep your mindset positive and focused, over time, you too will build the mental muscles necessary to achieve everything you desire. And then everything you desire after that. And so on.

You have to stay open and trusting. Don't let the components of the big picture define your attitude. Define your attitude to trust that the components you are given are only helpful ones. Your attitude can change them from blocks in the way to building blocks on the way. Your control is not over what components will show up. Your control is over how you define them. You can define them as bad for you or beneficial for you. Your definition will determine their role. A seeming setback could remain a setback or become a springboard that can accelerate you on your path. You hold the power. Your choice is not the current circumstances, but your attitude regarding the current circumstances. And that's how you filter the future circumstances.

What about Taking Action?

Now that we've talked about how your true control is not over the circumstances but tuning your attitude in a positive one, let's tackle the big question: what about taking action? If you are faced with a condition in your life, shouldn't you take action to resolve it, rather than go hide in the sand and work on your attitude?

When I was going to swimming lessons, I had a goal to learn to swim. I was taking all the actions that I could. I was showing up for classes. The moment I would go into the pool, I would be completely immobilized by fear. In panic, I would move my arms and legs to fight my way out of the water. The actions I was taking were as good as my current mindset allowed them to be. The result? I failed to learn to swim.

When, years later, I was in the water again, the circumstances were not much different. The same chlorine smell that triggered all my childhood horrors, the same water that I had to fight to survive. Yet, something was different: my attitude. When my life was on the line, I had no choice but to completely remove my attention from the unwanted. Death was not an option. It was my attitude that allowed the right actions to be taken. The result? I learned to swim. I lived.

The difference between taking action from a place of inner conflict or an action from a place of an aligned mindset is that one will keep you struggling, while the other will allow you to act on the opportunity and learn from whatever the opportunity quickly.

Your attitude defines your actions. When your attitude is away from the unwanted, you are inspired to the actions that support what you want. You may have noticed how you act when you are angry, fearful, resentful or generally unhappy. Those actions are very different from the actions you take when you are balanced and restored.

If apply your control to what you can, meaning your attitude, you will not be passive. You will be driven to take actions that support your goals. Even though it may seem that you have an unlimited amount of actions to choose from day to day, in actuality, the choice of actions has been already predefined and limited by your attitude.

Staying Fluid

Imagine you're a basketball player. You play a game, and you win! Afterward, you can watch the game back and analyze every move. You can pick out the good plays and the bad plays. You can clearly see what you could have done better or where you were potentially exposed.

Can you play this video before the game has started? The video doesn't exist yet. Neither does the game. It has yet to unfold. While you can see the full roadmap of what took place after the game, before the game has started, it's unknown territory. There is no way to plan what you will do in every second of the game. There is no way to control each specific detail in the game. Once the game starts, it is fast, dynamic, unpredictable and all you can do is adjust every moment to make a move that will support the final goal. If the opposite team scores, you groan and get over it. It is part of the game. You can't let it distract you. You have to maintain the right attitude and focus throughout the whole game. You can't control what each player does. You can't control what they think. All you can control is your attitude and focus.

It is similar with your desires. You can't see the whole game before it has unfolded. You can't control what will happen and how it will happen. But you can stay fluid and adjust to the circumstances as they come, maintaining your attitude and focus to support the final goal. Your attitude and focus will inspire the right actions at the right time. You can't let distractions or seeming setbacks distract you from your winning attitude.

The Question Words

English language has a set of question words that we use every day. You can use them every day in a slightly different way when it comes to your desires to help you navigate to what you can control and what you can.

WHO - you can't always control who's going to help you to have what you want. You have no control over what others do or think. You can't force a person to help you, even if you think they would be instrumental in your goals. Trying to control others only forces your attention into the unwanted. Plus, you may make people angry and upset. Nobody likes to be pushed to do or be something. The right people will show at the right times, often without anyone even knowing that they are what you need to successfully unfold your desires.

WHERE AND WHEN - you can't always control the exact place and timing of events. Impatience is the indication that your attitude is pointed toward the unwanted. There is a difference between impatience and anticipation. When you are impatient, you are tired of the wait. When you are anticipating, you just can't wait. One feels heavy and unpleasant, while the other one is joyful and happy. If you have wanted something for a long time, but it hasn't shown up yet, be careful not to get impatient or discouraged. Trust in yourself and your power. The fact that your goal is still out of sight doesn't mean it's not coming. Don't look at the distance between where you are and where you want to be. A big distance may discourage you and point you to the unwanted. Just take one step at a time. Taking one step at a time is infinitely bigger and better than taking no step at all.

There's no way to tell exactly when your desire will be realized. It's not like it has a tracking number that you can check on. Don't set a time limit for yourself. Don't keep the desire in a pending folder where you are constantly checking on a status update. In fact, sometimes removing your attention from your desire altogether for a while helps the mind immobilizing habits subside. It's still coming; don't try to time it out.

WHAT - you can't always control the circumstances. What you can control is your adjustment to the circumstances to make them work for you. When wind blows against a bird, it doesn't get mad at it. It adjusts its body position to take advantage of the current and use it to lift up. The bird can't transform the weather from windy to quiet. But it can transform what the wind represents to the bird in that moment. From a force against the bird, the wind becomes a force that helps the bird. It becomes a component that is beneficial for the mind environment, instead of a hostile setback. Like the bird, there are many things that happen in your life that you can't control. But you can control your attitude and see them either as disadvantages or as opportunities. You define them all.

"Don't let what you cannot do interfere with what you can do."

John Wooden

HOW - you can't always control how a desire is going to manifest in your life. I thought that for me learning to swim would happen by going to swim classes. Instead, my desire to swim unfolded in a much more wonderful and meaningful way that I will always remember and cherish. The wish came true, but not "how" I thought it would. There is no way for you to see the big picture. There is no way for you to see the opportunities that tomorrow will bring.

When I was struggling financially, I had no idea how I was going to pay for heat. I didn't know the "how" part yet, but I did know that I wanted heat: My fridge was warmer than the rest of my apartment for crying out loud. Could I have envisioned the person who approached me to form a company that was going to change things for me? Could I have predicted that an even bigger opportunity would very soon show up and I would win the Green Card Lottery, allowing me to be a permanent resident in the United States? Not really! I couldn't have taken those events into consideration when predicting the odds of my success, because they were invisible to me at the time. How did these miraculous things happen to me? I certainly couldn't control something as unruly as a lottery! It was just my attitude, my desire for a better life that I focused on. My focus and positive attitude created the "how" my success happened for me.

WHY - This question word is different from the rest. *Why* is the question that is completely within your control. Think about why you want what you are trying to manifest. Why you love the idea of it so much? Why it is important to you? Why will you be happier when you have it? In the answers to your "why's," you will be able to find the nuances that can build an attitude for success. The "why's" could be so beneficial that you may want to write them down.

Let's go back to our closet example. Here's two examples of Why.

I like knowing where my things are. (W)

I am tired of the clutter. (U)

If you noticed, one statement is marked with a "W" for wanted, and the other, a "U" for unwanted. The negative statements are the ones that point your attention to the unwanted end of the closet subject. The positive statements take you to the wanted end of the subject. Your job is to remove your attention from all the "U's." You can either reframe them, or take them out of your list altogether. By answering the question "why," you can define the thoughts that prevent you from switching from the problem to the solution.

It's not an accident that we use this closet example so much. For a clean closet, you first have to clean up the clutter in your head. The physical manifestation will naturally follow. Control what you can: your attitude. Don't take action with the purpose of controlling what you can't. You will be inspired to the right action in the right place, at the right time when you've taken care of what it is your job is to control. You are not the manager of the Universe (thank goodness, because that's a lot to put on one person's plate). Instead, you are the manager of your mind. And that's how you manage your Universe.

Stay Tuned to the Core Desire

The question words are great to use to catch yourself if you are trying to apply control where you can't. But there is more to it. It is very important to know what the core desire is. For example, you may want to win the lottery. So you check your desire against the question words. You don't care when, where, or what lottery you win. Great, those things are out of your control, anyway.

Now ask yourself why you want to win the lottery: the answer has to be, "I want more money." And this is where you have to be careful, as winning the lottery, in fact, is trying to control the "How" part. You are specifying that you want more money and that winning the lottery is how that money needs to happen. The thing is, a desire to have more money has its own unlimited potential to unfold through many different ways, most of which may be invisible to you at this moment.

When you try to limit in your mind the possible ways it can happen, you are wiping out all the other great possibilities that may be waiting for you, focusing only on the two remaining scenarios: winning or not winning the lottery. Beside, since not winning the lottery is a much bigger possibility than winning the lottery, there's a lot of room for you to focus on the unwanted of not winning. If you have the desire and the right attitude, more money will come. Let the endless possibilities flow over you. Stay tuned to the desire and don't worry about the specifics. Again, sometimes the unfolding happens in a way that is much more beautiful than what we could have envisioned. And that's the power of unlimited potential.

Try to find the core desire itself. You can do it by asking the question "why." In our example, if you want to win the lottery, the answer to the question would be to have more money. In fact, even the desire to have more money could be explored more with "why's." The why's may tell you that in your desires core, there is a desire for freedom, more time, ability to travel, ability to dress nicely, have a bigger house or have the latest technology in your home.

Trying to control what you can't is a mind immobilizer. Recognize it as such and know that it creates a habit of thinking that you are not in control of your life.

Fear of Failure

Failure can be a powerful tool that can lead you to success. In fact, one of the surest ways to reach a higher level of success is to use failure as a guide. If failure is accompanied by fear, though, the tool is useless. Fear freezes you into inaction. Fear makes failures seem like the end of the road, when in fact, failures are only road bumps that help you to understand the process deeper. What could be more valuable in learning what works than knowing what doesn't work? Then your next step can be better directed toward your desires.

When failure happens, it is not time to quit. It is time to stop and reap the benefits of the failure. It is time to dissect the cause-and-effects and gain better understanding of the process. From the new place of better knowledge, you gain a lot more in the long run. You become more powerful than before.

Death Valley holds the world's record for hottest measured air temperature: 134F recorded in July of 1913. [16] When I go there in the summer, I sometimes see a lot of identical cars, often covered in strange, squiggly patterns. A few times I've talked to the drivers, to find that these cars are prototypes of new models for large car manufacturers. For the last few decades, Death Valley has been the Mecca for car testing, due to its extreme heat. These tests are made with a specific purpose: the cars are pushed to the limit to look for possible failures. Studying when and how a car fails provide invaluable information, crucial for insights on improving performance. Millions of dollars are spent on car testing in Death Valley each year. One of the drivers I spoke to said, "If you want to make a premium car, you have to study failures from all possible angles and be prepared to spend some good money on it too."

Failure is not something to be afraid of. A lot of times we are afraid to follow our dreams and take action because the fear of failure is lurking behind the corner, reminding us that success is not secured. But think about it: Not taking action is the only thing that secures not reaching success. It's quitting before you even start.

We often have strange reasoning in our ideas about starting something new that we desire. When we want to invest, we base our investment on possible losses, not possible gains. But even if your investment does fail, it is still an invaluable learning tool to help you succeed in the next investment. You are already more successful than you were before, even with the failure. Don't be afraid! The paradox of the fear is that manifests itself as procrastination and avoidance. The fear knocks you off the path leading up to your desires and your wanted future. By having fear, you've already ensured the worst kind of failure: the kind that makes you quit before you ever try.

Failures are a good thing. Mistakes are data that can be gathered to help you understand the process better. Even if you've failed many times before, you've compiled good information that you can use to analyze what works and what doesn't. Failure helps us to move from surface thinking into deep thinking and increases our sights from what's immediately in front of us to what's off in the distance.

"The very first company I started failed with a great bang. The second one failed a little bit less, but still failed. The third one, you know, proper failed, but it was kind of okay. I recovered quickly. Number four almost didn't fail. It still didn't really feel great, but it did okay. Number five was PayPal."

Max Levchin, Cofounder of PayPal

I would like to look at one more aspect pertaining to the fear of failure. What if you are not smart enough? What if you don't have what it takes?

Let's imagine a scenario. How would you feel if your life was a series of failures and disappointments from as early as you can remember: you start school with high hopes but your teacher soon recognizes that you are not smart enough for school. After 3 months of trying, there is no more point in continuing, so you drop out. You get a job, but it's confusing and hard. To add insult to injury, you soon discover that you have hearing problems. Obviously, the answer is that you're not smart enough. Obviously, you were born disadvantaged. Would you give up trying to succeed? Thomas Edison didn't. His mom didn't believe the teachers when they said that her child was un-teachable. Instead, she chose to believe in her son and home-schooled him. Thomas Edison became a successful inventor and a businessman who is known all over the world for inventions like the phonograph, the motion picture camera and the practical electric bulb. Did he listen to the voice of his teacher? Did he think he was disadvantaged? Was he afraid of failure? He was asked once how he felt about his many failed attempts at making a light bulb. He replied, "I have not failed. I've just found 10,000 ways that won't work." And now, thanks to him, we can all have a light bulb moment.

You are as smart on a subject as the focus you've put into it. Nobody is smart in all areas. Some people are smart in science. Other people are smart in the way they find expression of their emotions. Some are smart in knowing how to be good parents. Some are smart in knowing how to maintain a home. Some are smart in relationships. Some are smart in arts. It all depends where the person has put their focus the longest, so that they can become better and better at it. When you focus on a subject long enough, you become attuned to it and soon more and more information is added to what you already know. It also becomes easier to go beyond your limit of knowledge and continue to get better. Would you judge somebody else as stupid because they don't understand your subject?

"Everybody is a genius. But if you judge a fish by its ability to climb a tree, it will live its whole life believing that it is stupid."

Albert Einstein

You have all that you need to start unleashing your potential right now. If there are things that you don't know yet, all you have to do is decide to learn them. With persistence, becoming good at anything is an achievable and attainable goal. You don't need to be born with a high IQ to be smart. Focus is all that you need. Lower down the volume of the distracting voices of fear and enjoy the ride. Nobody was born an expert.

Fear of failure is a mind immobilizer that creates a habit of thought that what you start, will fail.

Is Your Comfort Zone Getting Uncomfortable?

We all tend to stay within the range of our comfort zones where familiarity gives us a sense of security. When I was growing up in communism, there wasn't much for me to worry about. Education was free, including college degrees. Healthcare was free, including house calls. My parents' home was paid for, as was everyone else's. Salaries were within the same range with very little difference, regardless of the qualification. I had never seen a homeless person. I had never heard of someone who couldn't pay the bills. There was almost no crime. It was a very structured and secure system that covered all basic needs. It was a comfort zone that provided predictability and little surprises.

Yet, this comfortable security was not much different from a prison in the way that the basic needs were met, but freedom was limited. Information was scarce and censured. It was a closed market, so there was very little variety. We had the same clothes, the same furniture, and the same home layouts. Because there was no competition, quality was often questionable. If you went to a store, you would be faced with rows of boring and bleak merchandise. There was no motivation to make anything more appealing, because there was no competition. Religion or any kind of spirituality was out of the question. Our loyalty was not to be wasted on some intangible entities when it could be solely concentrated in worshipping the communist leaders and securing the longevity of the system.

The communist system gave a lot of security and predictability at the cost of personal freedom. It was a very stagnant environment where not much happened in terms of growth. Eventually, it couldn't sustain itself any longer and collapsed, leaving generations later struggling to rebuild their lives.

We all establish similar systems in our lives. They are similar in the way that they seem secure, but in reality we imprison ourselves within their limitations and our lives become stagnant, without much growth. A communist government forced my comfort zone limitations upon me; fear forced your comfort zone limitations on you.

The characteristics of a comfort zone are its lack of risks and its seemingly anxiety-free conditions. The boundaries of perceived security are actually the boundaries that limit our growth and progress. They also create limitations in the mind of what is possible. Anything outside the comfort zone is unknown, therefore potentially risky.

When communism crashed, we were forced out of the security of our comfort zone. Within days, the shelves in stores were emptied out completely. We were given ration coupons for all the basic necessities like groceries and gas. Standing in lines for hours was part of our daily experience. We had money to buy things, but there was nothing to buy. Then, all of a sudden, the stores filled up with fancy imported merchandise that we hadn't seen before. The problem was, our money had devaluated and now we couldn't afford to buy anything. The lines disappeared, together with our hopes that change was going to be easy. The system had stayed stagnant too long and we were paying the price.

They say the sky is the limit. In fact, the mind is the limit. If you want your life to change and become better, don't wish for it to be different. Wish for the courage to step out of the comfort zone. Once you're out, you can change your life yourself. Don't let anxiety or fears stop you from breaking out of your comfort zone. These are mind immobilizers and they will produce bad, stifling habits that keep you away from achieving your desires. Break out of your comfort zone, and you will find a happier, more successful life along the way.

There are three ways to step out of your comfort zone.

1.) Outside changes force your comfort zone's collapse.

2.) Discomfort of the limitation becomes bigger than the fear of facing the unknown.

3.) Your comfort zone becomes unnecessary, and so you discard it.

When your mind is powerful, not much can stop you from moving toward your goals. Your choices are dictated by fulfilling your desires, rather than fears. You are a free being, ready to explore more and more potential.

The first option: The most dramatic way to rid yourself of your comfort zone is when outside circumstances cause an abrupt change in your life, but it also carries the most potential for growth. In some cases, the change is something that you want, like winning a free vacation to Hawaii. In other cases, it could be a hurricane that forces you to leave home. Because of the intensity of the change, you are distracted from the fear of the unknown and you step into exploring what could be.

When you face unexpected changes, you obtain a new, broader perspective. Change becomes a possibility and often a choice. If it wasn't for the fear of leaving your comfort zone, how many wonderful things could you do with your life? How much different could you be?

In the Second option, change isn't forced on you: you define the change. Nothing limits you, except for your fears, and with a strong mind, something as ridiculous as fear won't get in your way. A strong mind would have no fear because it knows its power. The comfort zone is a confinement that you can willfully leave with the help of a strong mind.

When you step out of a comfort zone, what normally happens is that the limits of the comfort zone are pushed further. You accept what was once outside the limits as normal and you are able to operate with more choices and possibilities. This doesn't mean that you now have no limitations. Only they are pushed further, allowing you a larger territory of exploration. With each new goal and desire you make, you need to be prepared to push the limits again and again and not be afraid of the discomfort of stepping into the unknown. There are areas in your life where such changes happen naturally and without much fear. Think about the fast-paced technological evolution and the different changes that result from it. You easily leave the habitual behavior to allow the new, better ways of doing things. You are fully capable to handle and adapt to change when fear is not present. You can easily move the same way toward making your life better, when the mind is strong and not easily scared of the unknown.

Staying in your comfort zone is a mind immobilizer that creates a habit of thought that your personal expression and opportunities are limited within the rigid comfort zone parameters.

Release the Attachment to the Outcome

The ancient Taoist Chuang Tzu wrote about the split focus. An archer has his full skill until he shoots for a gold prize. Then the archer sees two targets. His skill is still there, but the prize divides him and drains him of his power.

There is a very fine line between focusing on your goal, while staying detached from it. It is in the detachment of your goal that the best unfolding happens and produces the best outcomes. Detachment doesn't mean that you don't want to achieve what you desire, but to be able to distribute your focus deliberately where it needs to be. This means that while you are doing what will take you to your destination, you have to be focused on what you are doing and put your attention in the present moment, rather than on the goal itself. The goal is still there, but your focus needs to be on the current activity or step to help you reach that goal.

The best creations in life are rewarding ones, not creations that are simply a means to an end. When we sincerely want to create, the creation of our goals becomes something we seek out, not merely a work obligation. When we do something out of obligation, our motivation suffers because what we're doing is not fun anymore. When something becomes an obligation, it becomes a threat to your autonomy. How much greater could your success be if it is supported by peak performance, rather than just an obligation? How much more personal expression could be unleashed if your personal autonomy was not threatened? You could have satisfactory results with obligation or exceptional results with passion.

The first time I tried to run in the morning, I set an easy goal. I was going to run only to the first stop sign on the street. After two minutes of running, I realized that the goal was still too far for my abilities. I quit. The second day, I tried again with the same results. After a week of trying, I was ready to give up running. Then, one morning, a great song came on Pandora, and I decided to listen to the music and not look at the stop sign at all. I focused on the pavement right in front of my feet and relaxed into the rhythm of the music. It was like a dance on the road. Even though running was still not easy, I was starting to notice a strange sense of enjoyment. I knew I wanted to reach the stop sign, but I was also okay if I didn't. In that moment, reaching the stop sign had become a non-issue. I was enjoying the moment. That was the day I reached the stop sign. And soon after, I was able to reach the stop sign after that. Running became a great morning pleasure for me.

There is famous study conducted in the 70s by Stanford researchers Mark R. Lepper and David Greene. Lepper and Greene selected a group of preschoolers who enjoyed drawing. They separated the children into three groups. The first group was told that they would receive a reward for drawing and asked if they would draw for the reward. The second group was simply asked to draw without any reward promises and after they finished, some of them were given a reward. The third group was asked to draw if they wanted to, but they were not promised or given a reward. Two weeks later, the researchers returned to the classroom, set out paper and crayons, and secretly observed the children's drawing habits. Out of the three groups, group one, the children who had been promised a reward for their effort, showed the least interest in continuing to draw. The pastime had devolved into work for group one, and no longer felt like a fun pastime. [17]

When the process becomes a means to an end, it negatively affects the high performance, the enjoyment of the activity and the creativity. It becomes a threat to your autonomy. What could be a very rewarding experience with great potential becomes a boring to-do list that needs to be checked off as soon as possible. It is a matter of switching the place of the reward. Instead of the goal being the reward, the experience in reaching the goal needs to be rewarding.

There are goals that don't need us to be in any special state of high performance or in the zone. Cleaning your house, for example, is a goal that you can handle regardless of the state of your mind. Of course, it would be great if you could fully enjoy cleaning, but it is a task that is relatively simple and achievable nevertheless. For simpler goals, or mundane activities, you don't need to worry about being detached from the outcome. You can stay focused on the reward to keep yourself motivated. For goals that require more time and openness to inspiration and hunches, it is good to keep the goal as background, instead of it being in the spotlight. The spotlight needs to be on the steps you are doing to reach that goal. That's where the best inspiration happens.

Processes to Help You with Mind Immobilizers

The mind immobilizers are not bigger than you. Because of their control-freak nature, they may seem like giants, but the truth is, their physical size is at least forty times smaller than yours. How do I know this? The brain-to-body ratio in humans is 1:40. And mind immobilizers are definitely smaller than your mighty brain. They are habits of thought that you've practiced for a long time: long enough to consider them a normal part of life. But they are not. They are only tracks in a grassy field that if not used, will soon disappear as new grass grows there. Now that you understand the high cost you pay when you let them run your life, most of the work in reducing the mind immobilizers to a minimum is done.

How long will it take to change your bad habits of thought to more beneficial ones? Well, in 2009, a study was published in the European Journal of Social Psychology. Each participant selected a behavior to repeat daily at the same time for twelve weeks. What they found is that for a behavior to become a habit, it takes an average of 66 days. What's more interesting is that the range of habit formation varied among the participants. The range was wild, from 18 to 254 days. In other words, depending on the habit that you are forming and your personality, the timing may be different.

The good news is that this is the time required for a behavior to become automatic. In the meantime, the new behavior will become easier and easier and will require less and less effort. Establishing the initial habit is what requires the most effort. As you keep repeating the same behavior again and again, the pathway becomes stronger and the behavior: easier. [18]

Don't Be Hard on Yourself

Never, ever, ever, ever be hard on yourself. Ever! The worst thing you can do to yourself, or to your manifestations, is to be hard on yourself. Stop judging yourself. You haven't messed up anything. You haven't failed at anything. You haven't done anything wrong. You are just mid-journey on your path, the way you will be for the rest of your life because of your ever expanding and evolving nature. Where you are now is perfect and exactly where you are supposed to be. It is a powerful platform that all your life has culminated into - a platform that has the potential for you to express your greatness. If there is something in your life that you don't like, understand that it is the unwanted part of a subject that has been activated. This is good! It means that you have generated a desire and the creation of something better has started!

While building new mind immobilizer free habits, you need to be careful not to be hard on yourself. If you experience a negative emotion, don't feel bad for feeling bad, as that will only shift your focus on what you don't want. If you were meant to only have positive emotions, you wouldn't have been given the skill to experience negative emotions. Negative emotions show you that your attention is pointed to what you don't want. When you first recognize that you have something that you don't want, it is only natural to have an emotional reaction to it. Don't suppress or fight the initial emotion that comes. If you do, it remains unresolved and suppressed and it will show up again in the future on the subject. If you have to cry, cry it out. Once you get your reasoning back, use the coping mechanisms in this book or other coping mechanisms that you've learned that help. There is nothing wrong with reacting to life. It only becomes a problem if it remains suppressed or unresolved and therefore chronic. Negative emotional reactions are not mind immobilizers. They only become mind immobilizers if they become habits of thought. A little bit of negative emotion could be motivating. A chronic negative emotion is immobilizing.

Thought Control

You probably don't think too much about polar bears in your daily life. But, if I give you the task not to think about polar bears in the next ten minutes, it will ensure that you won't be able to get the large animals out of your head for the duration of the task and even after.

If you find yourself thinking about polar bears and you can't get them out of your mind, don't worry. You are not the only one.

"Try to pose for yourself this task: not to think of a polar bear, and you will see that the cursed thing will come to mind every minute."

Fyodor Dostoevsky

Daniel Wegner, a social psychologist at Harvard University and the founding father of thought suppression research, decided to put this statement to a test with a simple experiment. He gathered a group of students and asked them to verbalize their thoughts, while being careful not to think about polar bears. If a polar bear came to mind, they were to ring a bell. Despite the instructions to avoid polar bears and despite the students' efforts, each of them thought of polar bears more than once per minute. Wegner ran other experiments which confirmed the same result: the more you try not to think about something, paradoxically, it makes you think of it more than if you weren't trying to suppress those thoughts. Something as innocent as a polar bear isn't such a bad animal to occupy your thoughts. It's when you try to suppress a tempting thought, or a stubborn fear, or a worry, that things get serious. The more you try to fall asleep, the more you are guaranteed to stay awake. The more you try not to think about the ice cream in the freezer, the faster your legs will take you there. The more you try not to think about your fears, the scarier your world becomes. Wegner found that trying to suppress thoughts often backfires and calls for even more intrusive thoughts on the specific subject. He coined the term "ironic mental processes" which is well known as the "polar bear phenomenon." But why does thought suppression act like a boomerang in that when you try to throw the thought away, it only comes back into your mind harder than before?

Wegner hypothesized that, for any other task, your brain knows how to handle it and stay away from a forbidden action. If you cut your finger and you have to avoid getting it wet, your brain can maintain the task of reminding you to stay away from water while you continue with your daily activities. It monitors for situations where you could get your finger wet and when it recognizes one, it alarms you to remind you to keep the finger away from water. You don't have to keep thinking about it. You've set the monitor to keep track of your actions and remind you when necessary.

When you tell your brain not to think about something, you are setting the monitor to keep scanning to ensure that you are not doing what you should stay away from. For the ten minutes that you tell yourself not to think about polar bears, to ensure that you are not thinking about polar bears, the monitoring system scans for polar bear thoughts. But because it is actively scanning for polar bears thoughts or ideas, it is constantly bringing polar bears to the surface. Thus, you end up thinking about polar bears. [19]

Another interesting thing that Wegner found is that the thought suppression backfired the most for people who are stressed out, depressed, tired, anxious, or distracted. In other words, they were in a weakened state of mind. Exactly the state you would be in when you are facing a mind immobilizer that you are trying to neutralize.

Accept

The way to control your thoughts is actually to give up control. You saw earlier how in order to point to what you want, you first have to remove your attention from what you don't want. The way to handle persistent habitual thoughts is to let go of control and accept the thoughts. Accept the fact that they are still coming and don't try to suppress them. The moment you try to stop them, you are adding power and next thing you know, you are thinking about those polar bears again. When the thought comes, instead of fighting them, you can just allow them to play out. Think about a toilet flush. You've pressed the lever and now there is nothing you can do to stop the water until it's done. It sounds contradictory, but when you give yourself permission to think a thought, it switches the roles and instead of the thought controlling you, you control the thought instead.

Observation and Breathing

If you are having unwanted thoughts, observe the thoughts without trying to control them. Notice if you can feel their resonance somewhere in your body and then turn your attention to your breathing. If you don't fight the thoughts, they will run their course and very soon leave you alone. Also, it is good to remember that not everything we think is true. Not everything we think needs to be acted upon either. We may not have control over the appearance of a thought in that moment but we still have a choice not to act on it. Thoughts are just established patterns in the brain. Put yourself in the position of an observer, rather than an experiencer. Observe the thought without judging it, as if you are curious to see how it will play out. This engages the Manager and switches to direct experience mode. The next time the thought appears, it will have less power over you.

Postpone

When a mind immobilizing thought comes and you recognize it, try to set it aside for 2 minutes later. Gradually increase the delay time. If possible, make the delay even longer, maybe a day, or a week. You are not prohibiting yourself from having a thought (which would make it stubbornly come back), you are just making the period of not thinking it a little longer. If you are worried about a future outcome, for example, tell yourself that you can worry about it in a minute. Then in another minute. Then in an hour.

Visualize

When a mind immobilizing thought comes, accept it and allow yourself to find where in your body you can feel it. Breathe slowly and deeply. While breathing deeply, visualize the thought as a cloud around you that you are blowing with your breath. The more you breathe the more the cloud disperses and disappears into the distance. Don't try to chase the thought forcefully out of your head. Once you've seen the image of the cloud, just visualize it dissipating. You've already established the connection between the unwanted thought and the cloud at the beginning. Your job is to visualize the disappearing cloud, not the disappearing thought.

P&L

Do a profit and loss analysis. Is this mind immobilizer giving you any benefits? How high is the cost? Remember, it is causing cognitive dissonance, which weakens you and has negative long-term effects. Is it worth it to give up your power for something that has no benefit to you? Is it worth the cost of weakened mind and diminished creative resources? Does it feel good? Can you find any benefit at all? Take a sheet of paper and separate it into two columns. In the first column, right the benefits of the thought. In the second, write the cost. Do this in writing, as writing it will help you to focus better and see it more clearly.

Perspective

Everything that happens in your life has the potential of being a stepping-stone for expansion and growth. What desires have you generated from the experience? Look at what you don't want and define what you do want. Now that you've defined the desire, do you want to have the desire happen or would you prefer to stay in the problem a little longer? Do you need to defend the problem? Are you able to change anything that has already happened? Are you able to control the future with the thoughts that you are having now? Is this situation giving you a good potential for improvement in your life if you turn your attention towards the wanted, rather than unwanted?

Cognitive Distortions

Cognitive distortions are irrational patterns of thought that make you perceive your world negatively and are often the basis for the mind immobilizing habits. Psychiatrist, Aaron T. Beck, laid the groundwork for recognizing cognitive distortions and his student, David D. Burns, further researched them. Read through the list and see if any of them are interfering with the way you perceive events in your life. They are all automatic thinking that you may have picked up earlier in your life that affects our point of view and clarity.

All-or-nothing thinking: this is seeing things in black and white. For example, if you fail at a job interview, you may think that you are a total failure. Or if you don't get perfect results in what you do, you may get a feeling that you are a complete loser. This type of thinking is unrealistic and causes you to be afraid of making a mistake because when you do, you will feel worthless. It involves using works like "always," "every" or "never" (It always happens to me; Every time I try to make a change, I fail; I can never get it right). This exaggerated way of thinking is not true. Nobody is perfectly successful at everything and nobody is an absolute failure at everything. If you look at the world in terms of absolute black and white, you can never measure up to your expectations. It would be impossible for anyone.

Overgeneralization: this is the tendency to make generalizations based on a single incident. If something bad happened once, it will happen again and again. If, for example, you spilled coffee on your new shirt, overgeneralization would be: "It always happens to me, this is just my luck. I always spill coffee on my shirts!" This, of course, is not true. The times that coffee was spilt is only a small percentage compared to the days you go stain-free.

Filtering: this is focusing entirely on the negative elements of a situation, completely excluding the positive. For example, if somebody was a loyal friend for years, but did one "bad" thing, you may find yourself focusing entirely on the negative part of the whole relationship. Or if you asked people for feedback on your new project, where you may get a lot of compliments and only one criticism, you may find yourself discarding the compliments and focusing completely on the critical opinion. This is not an objective way to look at things and your judgment could be clouded by only seeing one side.

Disqualifying the positive: this is the tendency to change neutral or positive experiences into negative ones. For example, someone may pay you a compliment and you may quickly disqualify this comment by thinking there is no grounds for their compliment. If you received criticism, on the other hand, you would dwell on it and take it as a proof that you are not good enough.

Jumping to conclusions: this is when you don't have enough information to make a conclusion, but you still make one, which is negative. For example, if somebody buys only diet soda for a party, when they know that you don't drink diet soda, you take it as a sign that they have completely disregarded you and you may feel like your voice doesn't matter. You may respond to those thoughts by changing your behavior at the party. In reality, the person buying the soda had a long shopping list and completely unintentionally bought what they are used to buying for their family.

Magnification and minimization: this is when you give a lot more attention to your failures, mistakes and imperfections, while giving little attention to your successes, strengths and victories. If you make a mistake, for example, it becomes the focus of your attention and you exaggerate its importance. Your strengths, on the other hand, are left in the background with hardly any importance given to them.

Emotional reasoning: this is when you think that your emotions are telling you the true nature of things. For example, you may feel overwhelmed and think that your problems are bigger than you or irresolvable. Or you may be mad at a friend; therefore they are wrong in whatever they say to you. However, your emotions distort the filter on reality. Your perception is not what's actually happening.

Should statements: this is a common distortion in which you expect others to do what you think they are morally obliged to do, disregarding the details of the specific instance. You could have thoughts that others owe you a certain behavior or that they should know what is expected of them. You could have the same thoughts about yourself as well. When the expectations are not met, this type of thinking creates a lot of unnecessary resentment for others and when it is pointed at you, it can trigger self-loath, shame and guilt.

Labeling and mislabeling: this is a stronger case of overgeneralization. It is taking an action of a person and applying it to their character, instead of seeing it as a situational attribute. You could do the same with your own actions and take one incident that you apply to your self-image as a whole. You may think that you are a failure, instead of thinking that you just made a mistake.

Personalization: this is taking responsibility or praise for events outside your control. For example, you may feel responsible for someone's bad mood. Or a mother may feel responsible if her child fails the test. This is a very immobilizing distortive thinking because it triggers a lot of guilt for events where the choice was not yours to make. You are not in charge of other people's choices or thoughts.

The list of cognitive distortions can help you to find the core issues of the mind immobilizing habits in your life. When you are experiencing an inner conflict, stop and recognize if you are actually having a distorted way of thinking. Recognizing it as a distortion will help you to question its validity and gradually gain back your clarity. [20]

Meditation

By now you understand the importance of a strong mind relative to manifesting your desires and pointing your attitude toward the wanted end of a subject. A strong mind will make your manifesting journey much more effortless, the way strong muscles make a strenuous hike an easy and enjoyable experience.

You know from experience that strong muscles are built by hard work and persistence. Luckily, that's not the case with building a strong mind. You can build a strong mind by doing something far simpler that only takes 5-10 minutes a day: meditation. The brain is like a muscle and meditation works that muscle the way that weight lifting pumps up your biceps. The returns on such small investment of time are enormous and life changing.

Neuroscientists have discovered that regular meditators have more grey matter in the prefrontal cortex - the area of self-control. Meditators also have more neural connections between the regions of the brain that are in charge of staying focused and ignoring distractions. In other words, if you meditate, you have the mind strength and the attention control to ignore the mind-immobilizing thoughts and successfully point your attitude to the wanted end of the subject. To you, this translates into would-be disappointments transforming into enjoyable journeys to your desired destinations.

You don't need to be a master meditator to experience the effects of meditation. In fact, five or ten minutes a day are sufficient to initiate changes in the brain. A very simple and easy meditation for you to participate in is focusing on your breath. Simple as it is, its effects are powerful.

1.   Take a seat where you feel grounded and stable. You can either sit in a chair or cross-legged on the floor. Rest your hands in a comfortable position; most people find that their knees or thighs, is the most comfortable position. Extend your spine so that you are sitting upright, but not stiff or tense. Close your eyes.

2.   Try to stay put. Don't fidget, adjust your body or scratch an itch. Staying still is part of what builds your self-control. You are training yourself not to follow every urge that comes to mind. Just feel the urge, register it but don't follow it.

3.   Pay attention to your breath. You don't need to force a rhythm in your breath; you just need to simply breathe in and out naturally and pay attention to it flowing in and out of the body. If your mind starts to wander (and it will), simply bring your attention back to your breathing without judging the experience.

You can start with only five minutes a day and gradually increase the time to up to thirty minutes. If you are not comfortable with more than five or ten minutes, keep your meditation at that.

What makes a successful meditation? The success of a meditation doesn't measure in the thoughts you didn't have. What makes the meditation successful is bringing your attention to the breath again and again. This is exactly what happens in life: distractions and mind immobilizers will come, but you bring your attention again and again on the desired goal.

Something else happens during meditation as well. While you are exercising your attention control by focusing and refocusing on the breath, you are also reducing the noise of the mind immobilizers. Mind immobilizing thoughts may come and go, but for the duration of the meditation, you purposefully ignore them and bring your attention back on the breath. Because your attention is away from the thoughts that bring your attention on the unwanted end of different subjects, and because attention to the unwanted end of a subject is what creates stress, meditation naturally reduces your stress levels. This is a highly beneficial and healing process with short and long-term dividends.

Challenging the Boundaries

What this power is, I cannot say. All I know is that it exists... and it becomes available only when you are in that state of mind in which you know exactly what you want... and are fully determined not to quit until you get it.

Alexander Graham Bell

Let me start with two stories, each taking place in different times and different places.

A famous study was conducted by Baylor School of Medicine, published in the New England Journal of Medicine. Participants were recruited from the Houston Veterans Affairs Medical Center. All patients suffered from moderate to strong knee pain. The purpose of the study was to evaluate which part of the current procedure was giving the most relief to the patients. The patients were separated into three groups. The first group was given one part of the procedure. The second group received the other part of the procedure. The third group was given a made-up procedure, where the surgeon made three incisions above the knee and washed the marks with saline. All three groups were given the same post-operative care: the same walking aids, the same exercise program, the same pain medication. Results were measured for the next two years.

It was expected that the patients from group one and two would show improvement. What was shocking was that the group three showed just as much improvement from their placebo effect surgery as the other two groups! What was going on? How was that possible? Could the mind have extraordinary power that we are not aware of? And why does placebo effect only work under certain conditions? [21]

In another part of the world, a thirty-nine-year-old alcoholic checked into the Charles B. Towns Hospital for Drug and Alcohol Addictions. This was going to be his fourth attempt to stop drinking. About a month earlier, he had seen an old drinking buddy who had managed to stay sober for several weeks. He was amazed. How could anybody manage to quit? He had tried himself. He went through detox and joined abstinence groups. None of it had worked. How did his friend do it?

"I found God," his friend said. Our alcoholic thought his buddy was crazy.

At the hospital, our alcoholic was given a hallucinogenic drug called belladonna, used at that time to treat alcoholism. While going through the terrible withdrawals, he called out: "If there is a God, let Him show Himself!" At that moment, he saw white light fill the room, the pain stopped, and then he knew that he was a free man. The name of the alcoholic is Bill Wilson. He would never have another drink in his life. The former alcoholic went from a ruined man to someone who was named in the "100 List of The Most Important People of the 20th Century" by Times magazine for co-founding Alcoholics Anonymous - the most powerful and successful organization to help alcoholics stop drinking and rebuild their lives. Millions credit the program with saving their lives. The famous twelve-step program is now successfully used to treat addictions like gambling, drugs, sex, smoking or any other addictive destructive behaviors.

What do these two stories have in common, a placebo surgery and a coming to God? Well, it illustrates that a person's belief produces an actual improvement of a condition, whether it's something physical like a knee injury, or mental, like alcoholism. What is it that makes some people susceptible to this effect? And what is it that triggers physiological changes?

Many studies and research have been done relative to the success of Alcoholics Anonymous. How could a program that has no scientific foundation have such high success rates? Not only that, but some of the aspects of the program seem strange, to say the least. In the program, members admit that they are powerless over alcohol and they need the help of a "higher power." They are to share their darkest secrets with someone else. Then they are to ask God to remove the defects of character and make amends with people they've harmed. They are asked to take continuous inventory of themselves, and hold spirituality through meditation and prayer. Finally, they are to carry the message to other alcoholics and help. [22]

AA members go through acceptance of their current situation, while building trust that there is strong support on their side. While doing their inventory, they go through healing the aspects that are immobilizing them and maintaining their inner health through regular meetings and helping others. All this is done in an environment of trust, loyalty, and support. Clearing the mind immobilizing habits builds confidence and belief in one's own abilities to change. Belief is the key ingredient to AA's success rate.

Belief doesn't have to mean belief in a God. As we learned in our first example, group three believed the surgeon's authority. Baseball players believe in superstition. Things they did the day they achieved victory will continue to lead them to victory, as long as the player maintains the belief in the superstition. It doesn't matter where the belief stems from. What matters is the belief itself. It is the capacity to believe that there is something out there on your side that is more powerful than you. We may not always believe in ourselves, but when we can trust that there is a power out there, supporting us on our path, things change. In times of fear, we hold on to the belief, reaching for the helping hand. This helps us to restore our balance again. It helps us to quickly point ourselves toward the solution. We may feel incapable of success, but we believe that something or someone else is. So, we give up trying to control what we haven't been able to control and stop our internal fight. We accept the situation and trust that it can be resolved.

Believing in something more powerful than yourself can be an important ally on your growth path. Whether you believe in one God, many gods, the Universe, the goodness in all of us, love, or higher order of things, having faith in the higher power can help you to endure stressful situations and feel connected to the bigger purpose in life. It is very beneficial to deepen your spiritual experience and faith.

This is what belief does: it allows us to relieve our conscious mind of trying to solve something that it can't. This, in turn, releases the grip on the current, unwanted reality and allows us to point our attitude toward the wanted outcome. By delegating the control to something or someone outside of us, we no longer need to keep our attention on the pending issue in an attempt to fix it. When the attention is removed from the unwanted side of the subject, the wanted side is activated and takes precedence.

In his book "Your Brain at Work," David Rock examines the power of expectations and the fact that they indeed produce changes in the brain. Considering that your brain is the filter that allows experiences to manifest or blocks them, your perception can actually change your reality. David Rock points out an experiment performed by Professor Robert Coghill, a pain researcher at the University of Florida. Coghill looked at brain scans of people whose pain expectations were altered. He found out that when people expected lower pain, but were given a higher dose of pain, the brain's response to pain changed according to their expectations, not according to the pain level. Meaning, these people were actually feeling quite a bit of pain—they just didn't know it, because they were told to expect a low amount of pain. So that's what they perceived. [23]

Not everyone can be cured with placebo pills. Only about 30% of the population seems to be susceptible to the placebo effect. Not all AA members remain sober either. AA's data shows that about 36% still attend AA meetings a year after their first meeting. The reasons are the complexities of our belief systems, as well as many factors that constitute our mind conditioning. There are many positive and beneficial beliefs that we hold. There are also many negative beliefs that we've picked during our life journey that don't serve us well. Your life responds to your beliefs. Your body responds to your beliefs. Your experience responds to your beliefs. And in the areas where you are a skeptic, your outcome is doubtful.

Mahatma Gandhi said it the best:

"Your beliefs become your thoughts

Your thoughts become your words

Your words become your actions

Your actions become your habits

Your habits become your values

Your values become your destiny"

The Guards of Your Belief System

Your belief system is very protective of itself. Once a belief is formed, it is stable and not easy to change. You can't just go into the beliefs database and start changing things as you please. You can't dig into your brain and change the belief "I am a normal person" to "I am superhero with special powers," or "The more donuts I eat, the more I lose weight." Your beliefs are stored cause-and-effect principles that your brain has adopted. Once they've been processed and adopted by your brain, they are stable and define your future experiences. A lot of those beliefs are unconscious.

Belief systems are protected by three main guards: Established Tracks, Confirmation Bias and Frequency Illusion.

Guard One: Established Tracks

Your beliefs are formed in many ways. During your childhood, you absorbed the beliefs of adults around you. They had been here longer, so they must know better how things work. Of course, once you become an adult yourself, you realized that adults are far from all knowing and that while you acquired a lot of good information from your parents, you also added their prejudices, fears and confusion into your belief system.

Your own experiences and interpretations play a role too. Most of your ideas about the world were shaped in the early years of your life and most of them will stay with you for the rest of your life. If you had a similar childhood experience several times over, your perception and reaction to the experience formed a well established pathway.

Established tracks are like a car going through a grassy field: the first time you drive through the field, the tracks are weak and if you don't repeat the same route, the grass will very soon cover the tracks. But if you drive there again and again, soon no grass grows in those tracks and you have an established road, and a solid pathway connecting a cause to a specific effect.

Your beliefs shape your actions and experiences. Some of your beliefs are good for your goals. Others may be working against your efforts. If you've been told that you won't amount to much in your childhood, trying to be successful in an area takes you on an expressway with a "Dead End" sign. If you've been told that you are smart and good at everything you do, trying something new takes you on a wide road network of possibilities.

As an adult, you continue to absorb beliefs through your experience and the information shared by people that you consider knowledgeable on a subject. New beliefs are formed as you watch TV and observe different cause-and-effect principles. You add beliefs through your interaction with others, through the materials you read or watch, through your observations of how the world works. If similar effects happen after a cause, you accept the cause-and-effect as valid and add it to your belief system. Acquiring beliefs is something that gives you efficiency, so you don't have to reinvent the wheel and form an original, from scratch opinion every time you come across a cause and effect.

The fact that there are established pathways does not mean that you are stuck with them. Neuroscience has proved that the brain is not static, but malleable. In fact, your brain changes as you learn new things every day. Your capacity to learn is greater than you think. New beliefs can be formed and solidified as new learned cause-and-effect principles. You can do this deliberately, or you do it without even being aware of it.

Guard Two: Confirmation Bias

Do you believe all your beliefs? What if some of your beliefs are based on questionable grounds? What if the cause-and-effects that you observed are not enough to provide data for a conclusion? What if the beliefs were based on your perception, with no substantial evidence of truth?

Digging into your belief system is not always easy. There is a term in psychology called "confirmation bias." It is the type of selective thinking that tends to prefer only what confirms your beliefs and avoids or ignores what contradicts the beliefs. We all do it. Even scientists, who are trying to be objective, tend to favor information that supports their hypothesis. We surround ourselves with people who think like us. If we agree with someone's beliefs, we most probably like those beliefs already. Our beliefs are the results of paying attention to things in unison with what we already believe, while ignoring information that challenges the existing beliefs. Because of this, if you want to change a belief, you can't just tell your belief system: "Please correct Item 24, Part 2, Line 38 in my Belief System Codex from "My headache goes away after I take a pill" to "My headache goes away after I eat a tiny bit of sugar!" In the world as you know it, sugar does not cure headaches. But if you're given a sugar pill unknowingly and told it's a pain reliever, the placebo effect will work effectively, as even though the information is false, to you, your beliefs are aligned.

We tend to believe only what is close to our general belief system and stay away from what challenges it. We also have a tendency to interpret new information based on our beliefs. If you believe that Area 51 secretly keeps aliens and alien spaceships, you will find enough evidence of it. If you disagree with that idea, you will find enough evidence against it. If you believe that humans are mean creatures, you will find enough information everywhere to support it. If you believe that humans are generally wonderful creatures, you will be open to anything that confirms that statement and blind to anything that says otherwise.

Do you think you are in charge of your memories? What if I told you that even your memories and what you recall are relative? Can the confirmation bias affect the way you remember things? In 1976, Mark Snyder and Nancy Cantor ran a study at the University of Minnesota. They created a fictional character named Jane. For a week, the participants in the study read about Jane. In some cases, she acted as an introvert. In other cases, she acted as an extrovert. At the end of the study, the researchers divided the participants into two groups. The first group was asked to decide whether Jane would be a good librarian. The second group was asked if Jane would be a good real-estate agent. The librarian group remembered Jane as an introvert. The real-estate agent group remembered her as an extrovert. Without them being aware of it, the confirmation bias had caused the participants to selectively remember the parts that matched their idea about Jane. [24]

Guard Three: Frequency Illusion

Imagine that you want to buy a new car. You've looked at many cars, but you've made up your mind on the new Toyota SUV. You've looked at it, you've studied its features, and you've even test-driven it. Then something strange happens. All of a sudden, you realize that there are Toyota SUVs everywhere. You open the newspaper and you see a Toyota advertisement. You go shopping and you see another Toyota SUV at the parking lot. You turn on your TV and sure enough, you see a Toyota advertisement. What is going on?

Psychologists call this phenomenon a frequency illusion. By being exposed to a certain stimuli, you've developed sensitivity to it, and so can recognize the stimuli more frequently in your surroundings. By putting your attention on the Toyota, you've primed yourself to see them. It's not that they weren't there before. They were, only you were discarding the information as irrelevant. [25]

Changing Beliefs

As you saw, your beliefs are guarded by a very strong protective system. Not impenetrable, though.

Before we start, however, let's look at the type of beliefs you can have in regards to any subject or action. You can believe the subject or action is impossible to achieve. You can believe the subject or action is possible for some people, but impossible for you. And you can believe the subject or action is absolutely possible for you.

Impossible Things

Through your life experiences, you have definitively decided some things are impossible, like riding a unicorn. That said: impossible things, like having a cell phone or a computer you can control with your mind, exist in the world you live in now, and would have been considered crazy before their invention. With this in mind, perhaps it's best to steer away from the mindset that there are impossible things out there for you.

Possible Things, Impossible for You

When you have a desire, perhaps like the desire to clean your closet, you generally have enough evidence to prove it can be done in real life. You just don't believe that it is possible for you yet. This is where most of your unrealized desires are. As soon as you gain your confidence and faith in yourself, things start unfolding. In this way, you don't have to change your whole belief system on the matter, just your belief that you can achieve whatever you desire to.

Possible Things, Possible for You

This is the best mindset to be in. When you know an action is possible, and you believe that you are the one who can make the action possible.

Harnessing Your Attention

Now that you've been introduced to the three guards of your belief system- established tracks, confirmation bias and frequency illusion, how can you make them work in your favor? Well, there is one "entity" in your brain that is higher in the chain of command and has authority over the guards. It is your attention.

Let's say that lately you've been really irritable. Even though you don't want to be irritable, it's hard when there are so many annoying people around you. Let's take the grocery store, for example. You go there and you see a lady by the tomatoes, squeezing every tomato in the pile. You know the type. You call them the "tomato squeezers!" You pull out your smart phone and change your FB status to "Can't stand tomato squeezers!" Then you go in line at the cashier, and the guy behind you is talking on his phone super loud, while he's standing way to close.

What happened in the grocery store was that you only noticed the most annoying traits of people. And by continuing to do this, you prime your brain to only look for annoying habits in others. It is not the annoying people that are annoying. It is your choice of putting your attention on something that upsets you. You are not making them disappear by getting mad at them. You are not making your shopping better. You are voluntarily choosing self-torture.

What others do or think is outside of your control. You can't do anything to make them be who you want them to be. What you have control over is your attention. You can let it pick only the experiences that you like and ignore the rest. You can consciously start to point your attention to the people that you like. Notice the person who lets you in front of them at the cashier. Notice how orderly the store is and how easy it is to find what you want. Notice the people who smile at you for no reason at all, just because your eyes met. Just like you don't put everything you see in the store in your shopping cart, but make your choices selectively, you can use your attention to only observe what makes you happy. At first, this may require effort, but it will get easier with time. The more you consciously direct your attention to what you want to see, the more you will see it. And this is where the belief system guards start working for you.

First, the frequency illusion will kick in. The more you observe goodness, the more sensitive you become to recognizing it. You may start seeing things that you have not even noticed before. The more you see it, the more you solidify your belief in the goodness of people around you. Then confirmation bias kicks in. People who don't share your beliefs will be filtered out, similar to the way you filter out irrelevant information all the time. Soon, your manifestations will start representing the new filter through which you see your world. You can do this with anything. You can increase your sensitivity for things that work, rather than things that don't work. You can start remembering your own power.

As you can see, your attention is a very precious commodity. There are other people out there who already know this. Commercials, for example, send millions of dollars a year, just to catch your attention. News channels pick stories that they think will hold your focus. Even your friends will choose topics of conversation they know you will be engaged in. By taking a hold of your attention, these people are able to guide it to the destination they want for you i.e. buying their product, watching that TV channel, paying attention to their story, etc. Instead, focus your attention on yourself. Guide your own attention to what you desire.

The Secret of Hypnosis

Have you wondered how come somebody could be hypnotized and all of a sudden, they quit smoking, or they gain confidence, or they make a change they haven't been able to make before?

Let's start with the induction process. For someone to get into hypnosis, the hypnotherapist has to induce them into a hypnotic state. Often the induction is a relaxation technique, where the person being hypnotized is guided to focus on something that is relaxing and pleasant. There are many different techniques for induction: progressive relaxation of the body, counting down, shocking the person into a different state, or just by introducing an engaging story that evokes pleasant thoughts. During the induction process, the focus is placed on the words said by the hypnotherapist and taken away from the daily worries, feelings of guilt, blame, or fears. In other words, the hypnotherapist works so that all the distractions in your mind are removed. There is no active fight-or-flight response and so the mind is quickly taken away from healing mode, into growth mode. You are not pointed toward the unwanted and therefore you can make an easy and quick attitude switch to what you want. You are mind-immobilizer free at the moment.

When a distraction free state of mind is reached, the control of your attention is much stronger. Some call hypnosis a state of hyper-attention. The attention is not distracted in any way and can be easily pointed toward change. Even though the time in hypnosis is short, it is enough to start changing patterns. Add to this the belief that something or someone outside of you with better capacity to solve your problem is helping (the hypnotherapist, who is an authority in the field) and you have a relatively strong expectation for success.

Other than being under hypnosis, when you are calm and rested, controlling your attention is a lot easier. That's the time to gently guide your attention into a direction that is different from the established path. Read materials that support your new belief, deliberately select what you are watching or where you are directing your attention. Make a point to notice success patterns around you. Once you've decided to notice them, you will see them everywhere: in modern technology, in the perfection of how nature works, in the perfection of how your body operates, in our road systems. That's when small new habits are created and small victories are won. When you are upset, it is not the time to try to focus your attention. It is time to leave it alone, accept the fact that you've stepped into healing mode, relax about it, and allow the moment to pass. Don't be mean to your attention for all of a sudden finding yourself in healing. Nothing has gone wrong, as long as you relax about it. It's like flushing the toilet - once you've pushed the lever, you can't stop the flush. You just let it pass. When you are calm again, you can go back to your deliberate ride. The best control you have over your attention is in a calm state. Otherwise, it's like a horse gone wild. You may have some success in reining the horse in, but you may also get thrown off, leaving you with an impression that you are not in charge.

Since your attention is the most important factor that determines your life journey, the more you free yourself from mind immobilizing habits, the more you have general control over your attention and your life. You just have to understand that there are times you can control your attention better and times when it is much harder. Make sure to use the most of the times when you are calm to change your habits and the directions of your thoughts. By reducing the mind immobilizing habits, you increase the amount of time that you have control. That's when change happens.

Here are some of the things that make your conscious control of your attention weaker:

1.   Mind immobilizers

2.   Physical illness

3.   Abuse of toxic substances

4.   Not enough sleep

5.   During strenuous or demanding physical exercise

6.   Post-exertion of mental or physical effort

In any of those cases, don't be hard on yourself (if you are, you are activating cognitive dissonance, which makes you even weaker), and accept that this weak hold on your consciousness will pass and try to do what's necessary to relax and restore your strength in the meantime. Once you are back in a better balance, you can get back on that horse.

Belief is Contagious

Let me start with an anecdote. Will is sitting at home trying to do some work at his computer. A whole bunch of kids are playing outside with a ball and no matter how much he is trying to ignore them, it is driving him crazy. He needs to find a way to get rid of the kids. So, Will comes up with a lie, walks out and yells:

"Kids haven't you heard? They're giving away 100 free iPad Airs in the next hour on 3rd and 5th! Hurry!"

Without hesitation, the kids rush toward the freebies, while texting all their buddies and posting the news all over Facebook. Will is happy for the moment, as he has achieved peace and quiet. But then, other kids start rushing out of the houses on his block. One of the kids notices Will and says:

"Hey, man, they are giving away free iPad airs two blocks from here!"

Then adults start to leave their homes, telling him about the freebies. Will stands there, watching people rushing to 3rd and 5th and he starts to think, "What if they really are giving away free iPad airs?"

Without thinking about it, Will starts running as fast as he can to get there before they run out.

The opinion of a crowd affects us more than we may realize. Have you noticed that when somebody smiles during a conversation, you tend to smile back? We often find ourselves mimicking the physical gestures of the people around us. In fact, people in a conversation will naturally start adopting each other's positions. This creates a sense of connection. This is not an accident: to support our social nature, our brains are hardwired to connect with others. In fact, there is a group of neurons in the brain that are specifically assigned to mimic others.

They are called mirror neurons. Their task is to observe the behavior of others and "mirror" it, as if we are the ones doing the activity.

Mirror neurons are the reason why when somebody cuts their finger, you immediately think "Ouch!" Or if somebody is eating a juicy apple, your mouth may start watering, almost tasting the sweet, crispy, fragrant apple. Your brain knows that the secret to understanding people is watching their body language. While watching the activity, the observer is actually feeling something of what the other person is feeling. In a way, the mirror neurons help us to read other people's minds. By knowing how others feel, you know to some extent what others think. Mirror neurons help us understand other people's intentions by their actions, and they help us to connect with others by creating empathy.

It is a very common thing for us to mimic each other's behavior, even goals. If you and a friend go shopping at the mall and she is buying like crazy, you may find yourself taking out your credit card more that you had planned. If your friends or coworkers go on a diet together, you will be more likely for you to stick with your diet, too.

Have you wondered why so much canned laughter is used in TV programs and shows? The viewers very well know that this is not a natural laughter and it often comes after the least funny jokes. But it is a fact that audience will laugh longer and rate the jokes as funnier when canned laughter is played. Why is your judgment influenced by it?

One of the ways we determine what is correct and normal, is to look at what other people think is correct and normal. The more people around us consider a certain behavior as normal, the more normal it is for us. The more people consider an action appropriate, the more we determine its appropriateness as part of our understanding of how to behave. If a lot of people are doing something, it must be right. This mechanism is neither good, nor bad. It ensures that we fit into our social group and we won't be rejected. It gives us a sense of security.

Fitting in is also an efficiency management process that saves us a lot of time of reinventing the wheel with how to act and what to do in certain situations. In most areas, shortcuts are great. In areas where you would like to grow, however, it is worth it to step out of the influence of others and instead of being an imitator, become an initiator who listens to their own voice instead. [26]

How is this related to changing beliefs? A very powerful factor that affects your beliefs is your social surroundings. You are always being influenced by your surroundings, whether you consciously realize it or not. This, in turn, affects your general attitude toward your goals. The habits of thought define your beliefs.

If some of those acquired beliefs are not beneficial for you, you don't have to scratch the people out and never communicate with them again. It is enough to be mindful of how your beliefs were formed. This will help you to start looking for different answers. You can't cut off all your relatives and friends, just because they think that what you are trying to accomplish is impossible. But maybe you could talk less about what you want to do around them and start trusting your own judgment, instead of laughing with the canned laughter. The fact that something seems impossible to some, doesn't mean that it is. Everything is impossible until it's done. It all starts with a vision and reaches completion by fearless focus.

A good way to change a belief on a specific subject is to find people who have succeeded in it, or have succeeded in a similar area. By observing their success, you are starting to shift your perception from impossible to possible. Remember the AA meetings? A very powerful factor for change is listening to the stories of those who have made it. The group helps the individual by the momentum it carries and by the social environment that influences the beliefs. You could join a local club on the subject of your interest, or find meetings that are done by people in the specific area. Highly successful people often have met someone from their own social group who achieved success.

Sometimes, meeting people who have succeeded in your area may not be possible at the moment. If this is the case, you could deliberately narrow down your focus to watching and reading materials that support the new belief that you are trying to cultivate. Maybe you could find online groups that can give you the support. Or maybe find a podcast that inspires you. Your attention has more power than what you may be giving it credit for. Where it goes, your attitude follows. Use that power to your advantage. Build your mind environment by being careful about what outside environment you choose. According to social psychology, behavior changes often come before changes in the attitude. By being selective about your outside environment, you are making the change in your mind environment much easier.

Changing Patterns

Your brain likes to work in patterns and apply existing patterns to new situations. You can take advantage of this by introducing new, beneficial patterns that start spilling over other areas and situations. When people start exercising regularly, for example, they start changing other, unrelated patterns in their lives. This is often an unconscious process that starts without any special intent. They may become more confident, more organized, more selective in their food choices, kinder to their friends, or less prone to go for instant gratification. A new pattern causes widespread shifts and breaks the established limitations.

Witnessing success in any area affects the patterns of belief. The same applies to witnessing your own small or bigger victories. When you observe your success, it changes the way you think. Don't be shy about giving yourself credit. Celebrate even the smallest accomplishment. By changing one little habit successfully, you are altering a pattern that affects other areas in your life. The small victories are more important than we may give them credit for. They are keystones to widespread changes. Maybe you can start making your bed in the morning, or start an exercise routine, or for a week, try deliberately to notice the good in people around you. Even a change like switching the hand you use to brush your teeth in the morning sets into motion a change in your patterns. Small wins are key. They create the general beneficial thought environment for bigger victories. They help you to believe that bigger achievements are possible. They are the ones that set a climate in which all kind of new ideas are possible.

Visualization

It is very common for athletes to use visualization when they are learning a new move. Once they've been introduced to the move, they stop and concentrate on the move in their mind. They rehearse it again and again, visualizing each movement of their body. There is a region in the brain that is activated when we imagine a body movement. When athletes visualize, they are creating pathways as if they are actually doing the movements with their body. When they are ready to perform for real, their body follows the mind and the move is easier because the pathways in the brain are already in place. The practice of visualization has been found to be a highly successful tool for athletes.

Can you use the same type of mind mastery to change your life? What if I sat you down next to an experienced athlete and gave both of you the same task: to visualize in your mind doing a back flip - a move that neither of you have done before. Both of you will rehearse the move in your minds for the same amount of time. When your visualization assignment is completed and I asked each of you to do a back flip for real, do you think that you and the athlete would have the same results? In fact, do you think you will be able to do a back flip at all?

For the athlete, the visualization is an area that he is very familiar with. The athlete already has built up the muscle density needed to perform the backflip, he has body control, and he has prior experience - and success - in visualization. You, on the other hand, are visualizing new territory. Even if you find you have the focus to mentally prepare for the backflip, you may not be physically prepared for the strength it takes to perform the trick.

In other words, what is a short journey with little growth for an athlete may be a longer journey for you. You may have to catch up in growth and personal change. For you, a new idea was introduced in an old physical and mental condition. To realize the back flip, you will have to change.

When you have a desire, it is an active subject for you. The lack of what you want has put the subject in the foreground. As the subject has already been activated, you don't have to go out there and look for what you want. You don't have to buy a huge magnet to attract it. It's already active and therefore ready to start reaching its completion, as soon as you reach the growth that can allow it to unfold.

You have to become a new you before you can manifest the change in your life. What you want is not separate from you. You are not making anything happen. Instead, you are changing yourself to allow things to happen. When your parents bought you shoes that were one size bigger, you grew into the shoes. You didn't manifest shoes that fit. That's how you get what you want. You grow into what you already have. When the athlete visualizes the back flip, he grows into a person who can perform a back flip. He is not going out there to look for the back flip. The back flip is already his, by activation of the subject.

It's All About You

When the athlete visualizes the back flip, he is seeing himself different. You may want to have a bigger house. Although the desire is ready to grow into the new house, the key to your new house is not in your focus on the house itself when you visualize. It's in the focus on how you will be different if you had the new house. The thing is, it is much easier to picture a new house because new houses are something that you have seen. Picturing yourself having a new house is a little more difficult because you've never been there before. This is not much different from the caterpillar not knowing what it would feel like to be a butterfly. You may have an idealistic picture of how you think you will be if you had what you wanted. You may think that nothing in life could make you happier than owning a new home. The reality is, the excitement of having what you want quickly subsides because it becomes part of your normal reality. It is not much different from you getting a job you applied for. At first, the job represents victory. A month later, it is a normal part of your life. And that's what you want to reach for: how will you be once what you want has become part of your normal reality.

Build the Bridge

The goal is to grow into the person you would be if you had what you want. Because a lot of the future is still unknown to you, you will have to build a bridge that connects your current reality and the future you.

On the future side, if you had what you wanted, there would still be things that you would have to do, like go to the grocery store, drive your car in traffic, brush your teeth, talk to people, have a relationship, or fall asleep at night. These are experiences that are in your life with or without what you want. We will use them as a bridge. We will call them "bridge experiences." In your mind, visualize these experiences, but instead of seeing them through your current eyes, start asking yourself questions. If you had what you want, how would you be if you were stuck in traffic? Would you be calmer, happier? How would you be around your home? How would you be when interacting with other people? How would you be with your loved one? How would you be different? How would the world look through your future eyes?

When you look at the bridge experiences from your future self's eyes, focus the most on the way you feel in such situations. Find the emotional equivalent for what you want. The emotional equivalent to what you want is you being emotionally resolved on the subject. How would you feel and act if you were emotionally resolved on the subject of your desire? Put as much focus and detail into it as you can and see yourself in your visualizations being that person in bridge situations. If your relationship with your partner is not that great and you want to improve it, how would you be different if you were emotionally resolved? How would you be at your best? In your mind's eye, see it all. See your best self on the subject. How will you act in familiar situations? Will you smile when you go to bed? Will you wake up with a smile? Will you be kinder? Will you be more loving? Will you love yourself more? Will you be more at peace with the world? Now that you are creating the pathways for the resolved you in your brain, you can start projecting the same feelings in your current life. Just like in order for you to do a back flip you have to do some work at the gym in addition to your visualization, you can start working those emotional muscles in present situations. Reach for your emotionally resolved self on the subject in everything you do. What would the best version of you do? As any new habit, it will take practice. Don't give up. You have nothing to lose by investing a little time and effort, but a lot to gain. You have a whole life of manifesting ahead of you!

When and Where to Visualize

As you've learned so far, to grow into the person who has achieved your goals, you have to reach for the emotional equivalent of success. When you are in fight-or-flight response, you tend to see circumstances and people more negatively and you may incorrectly perceive them as threats. This affects your visualization because now you are visualizing from the lens of fear. This is an emotionally unresolved place where you have the critical filter on. You need to be in a calm state to visualize.

That's when you go to your quick and powerful relaxation tool: before you go into visualization, take a few deep breaths - as deep and long as you can. This puts your brain in direct experience mode and interrupts the mental chatter. It also evokes the relaxation response. Then pick a favorite place where you normally feel relaxed and happy. See this place in your mind in full detail. Engage all your senses: what does it smell like? How does the air feel on your skin? What are the sounds around you? Look around and pay attention to every detail that your mind can construct. Now imagine yourself finding a comfortable place where you can sit or lie down in this place. Consciously start relaxing all your muscles starting from your feet and moving up to your head. You may imagine a light touching and massaging each muscle. After you've relaxed, you may imagine a large screen with changing numbers, counting down from ten to one. Watch the numbers on the screen and with each number think "I relax." Once you've reached one, you are ready for your visualization. Now you can start seeing yourself in the bridge experiences through the eyes of the future you.

This short relaxation is very similar to hypnosis induction, only you are the one that is in charge. It clears the mind immobilizing thoughts, keeping you focused in a state where you feel relaxed, safe and concentrated. In such state, you achieve hyper-attention so you can have quicker results. Because you've temporarily released all emotional weight, you can take this time to reach for higher emotional states.

While this is a great relaxation to prepare you for your visualization, it is not the only time you can visualize. You can visualize when you are relatively calm, in any situation in your every-day life. You can do it while stuck in traffic or while you take your morning shower. Imagine you are your future self next time you go grocery shopping. You can start practicing being the better, expanded version of yourself anywhere.

Using Metaphors in Visualization

As you learned earlier, your brain likes to work in patterns. It uses patterns to understand the world and it applies existing patterns to new situations. Because of this, metaphor is an excellent way to achieve successful visualization. When you use a metaphor, your mind finds ways to connect it to your current belief system. You saw how your brain is very protective of your beliefs. A metaphor allows you to bypass the guards because you are not asking your brain to believe something that it doesn't. You are only introducing a story. Yet, the brain naturally makes the parallel between the story and your own life, reconsidering its old patterns. If, for example, you have a lot of fears in a situation, you can envision yourself as a tiger, walking powerfully and confidently. As a tiger, you can walk to a peril and fearlessly overcome it. You are not telling your brain that you are courageous, forcing it to relearn everything it's established. But you are allowing it to pick the pattern of courage from the story and apply it to your mindset during visualization.

You may believe that what you want is generally possible, but not much will happen until you start believing that you have the ability to make it possible. You have to be willing and able. The metaphors help you to regain the innate inner belief that you can create your life. Remember, what you want has the potential to be yours by means of having activated the subject. You only need to grow into your want to unleash the potential. Metaphors are great for releasing conscious or unconscious mental blocks, fears, or bad habits. They allow a new you to emerge, a person who has the power to reach their destination.

Before you envision a metaphor, you still have to go through the short relaxation that you learned. You need to be calm and focused. You can use your imagination to create any metaphor story that you want. Sometimes you may have to do the same metaphor more than once, depending on how engrained the habit of thought is. I've outlined a few guidelines to help you in creating an effective story.

Action Metaphors

In action metaphors, you take yourself to a place or a situation where you are about to take action to change the environment in some way. You may release burdens, open doors, tear down walls, cross a bridge or anything that symbolically represents permanently abandoning one behavior and changing it for a more beneficial one.

1.   Burdens: you can use this metaphor to release burdens that you've carried for a long time, like maybe guilt or blame. The burden can have any shape that your imagination likes: bricks, heavy rocks, a heavy backpack. The release location is also your choice. You could carry the burden to a higher place in order to feel how much it strains you and then throw it off a cliff. You can walk on a bridge and throw it in the water. You can simply leave it on the ground and move on. You can talk to your burden, if you want to. You can thank it for the lesson and tell it that it no longer serves you. Anything that symbolically represents the release.

2.   Doors: you can use this metaphor to leave a state of mind or a lifestyle that you don't want anymore, including addictive behavior. The goal is to walk through the door. You can see yourself in a small room, your comfort zone, where you are not fulfilled anymore. You can make the room small, dark and limiting, so that you can feel the contrast when you walk out of the door. Open the door to come out into the light, run free and in your mind, focus on the sensations of libration and joy. You can also use a door or a gate as a representation of stepping into a new place of awareness. You can see a beautiful gate, leading to a special garden where you are safe, secure and you can allow yourself to be loving, kind, happy and generous. You can imagine a secret sanctuary where your higher self can go and have fun. You may imagine cascading waterfalls, beautiful gardens, fountains, birds or anything that your inner designer of magical places

can come up with. This will help you to connect better with your higher self and intentions.

3.   Walls: you can use this metaphor to tear down the mental blocks that stand in your way. You can create a nice adventure story by maybe imagining yourself walking on a path in a beautiful forest. You come to a point where you can't go any further because there is a solid brick wall. To make your story more fun, you may look around for tools or help from others to tear down the wall. You may find a huge hammer, or some helping magical creatures. The goal is to see the obstacle and then find a way to remove it.

4.   Showers, waterfalls: you can use this type of metaphor to wash away stress, pain, emotional toxins, self-loathing, or criticism and blame. You can envision yourself as covered in mud or dirt, then walking to a beautiful waterfall that can wash it all off. You can swim in the pool of water, feeling the relief and enjoying the crystal clear water.

These are just a few examples. You can use your imagination to create any story that you want. Anything, as long as it helps you release your full potential.

Reframe Metaphors

This type of metaphor takes an observation of a process that relates to your experience. For example, if you are trying to overcome a loss, you may imagine writing something in the sand, then watching the waves gradually wash it away. Your brain will pick up the relation between the writing fading out and the pain, helping you to release your fears, accept what you can't change and know that the pain will gradually wash away. If you are going through difficult times, you can envision birds with wind blowing against them. The birds use the current to lift up, instead of being scared.

Parts Metaphor

This metaphor allows you to talk to different parts of yourself. You can take your fears, set them in a chair in front of you and talk to them. You ask them to leave, or you can ask them why they have been with you. You can talk to your courage, your concentration, or your gratitude. You can talk to your addictions or your health issues. You can guide the conversation any way you like.

Use your imagination to come up with any metaphor in your mind. You can use the metaphor to clear your mind, search for solutions, release old traumas, deal with chronic mind immobilizers, or anything else that you feel needs to change about you. Have fun with the stories and remember it's all about changing you, not the world around you. It's also all about the happy end where you find an emotionally resolved place.

Even though metaphors are not true stories, they have a powerful effect on the patterns in your brain. They help you to shift your beliefs and grow confidence in your abilities. They help you to remember who you are: a powerful, wonderful being loaded with potential to do or be anything you want.

The Blueprint

Have you ever thought about how many different things you've held in your hands throughout your life? How many things you've come in contact with? Some of them you've long forgotten. Memories of others may be special and dear to you, like holding a loving hand, or a sweet little baby, or a gift someone made especially for you. How many things have touched you in your life?

I've held many things in my hands. However, there is one very special thing that I want to tell you about. It is one of the tiniest things I've ever touched. This thing is not even a full centimeter long. It doesn't look like anything special; It doesn't glitter, it doesn't move, it's not particularly beautiful. The thing I want to tell you about is the sequoia seed.

If you looked at a sequoia seed, you would see nothing but a very ordinary dark brown little seed. The story that it carries and the blueprint that it holds, however, are more than impressive. This little seed knows what it will become. It already has the whole information within itself for its gradual and steady growth into the largest tree by volume on our planet. Some of the largest sequoias measure over 35 feet in diameter and up to 300 feet in height. 35 feet in diameter is the length of two sedan cars one parked right behind the other! 300 feet is the average height of a 30-story building! This tree is a giant! Yet, all this future unfolding of this giant is contained in nothing but a tiny little seed that you can hold in your hand. [27]

The sequoia seed contains the whole blueprint for what it will become. You could imagine holding the seed in your hand and a large, blue, high-tech hologram coming out of the seed, representing the tree at its peak. This bluish high-tech hologram is a visual tool for you to imagine what does exist - the information of the future giant that is contained in the seed.

A new desire is like a tiny seed. Even though the desire is small at the moment, it contains in itself all that is necessary to produce what you wish for. The Universe has already provided everything you want, just like that. Similar to the genius of the seed, knowing how to grow branches, how to grow a trunk, how to grow roots and all that is necessary for expressing its full potential, your desire contains in itself all that is needed for your wants and desires to unfold.

Not all sequoia seeds become huge sequoias. Some die young, others never even have a chance to sprout and initiate their existence. You don't need to be a master gardener to understand what seeds need. The right soil, the right nutrients, the right moisture, the right temperature and - voila! You have a giant in the making. Throughout its whole life, the tree will need the right climate and soil to continue to grow. Your desire seed is not that different. I am sure that you have plenty of desire seeds that you've already generated during your life. You can imagine a virtual room full of virtual small containers with different seeds. For some, you may have provided the right conditions. The desires have sprouted and you are now enjoying their growth. Others just sit in those virtual containers, waiting for you to prepare the conditions for them to take off.

Your desire seed has within itself the whole blueprint to put you in the right place at right time to make your wish a reality. Like a GPS, it has prepared different routes to take you to your destination. And just like a GPS, when you deviate from the route, it doesn't give up on you and call you names, but immediately recalculates the route from your new location. Once a desire seed is created, the whole Universe is ready with maximum support to take you to your full growth potential. And when the mind conditions are right, the path to your desire easily and effortlessly unfolds.

You learned that the right conditions for your desires are having the three components - desire, attitude and belief – all pointing in the same direction. You learned that what gets in the way of your attitude are the mind immobilizers and the general mind environment they create. You also learned that through changing your inner and outer environment, you are able to change your beliefs. You learned that when you reach the emotionally resolved you on a subject, you have set the right attitude for change.

Let's recap:

By recognizing that there is something that you don't want in your life, you activate a subject with its two opposites: wanted and unwanted. While the attention is split between the wanted and the unwanted, you may experience stress. As long as the stress is short-lived, it serves to motivate you to change. If the stress is not short-lived, there may be mind-immobilizing habits that are weakening you on the subject.

In order to allow the personal growth necessary for your desire to unfold, you have to be aware of these mind immobilizers and reduce them as much as possible. Be a Manager and observe your internal processes. The goal is to reach emotional resolution on the subject, as well as maintaining a healthy mind environment for your goals. Once you reach emotional resolution on a subject, your attitude is set and you are soon inspired to the actions that will take you to the successful completion of what you want. Now let's put it all to action.

This is a "quick start" to simply remind you not to wait until tomorrow or a future day. Start now. Start quickly.

1. Perform a full system clean up. Even the best computers will run slowly if they are infected with viruses. The goal is to reduce the mind immobilizing habits to a minimum. Do a quick scan of when your mind immobilizers are activated and work on decreasing their presence in your system. Monitor the times when you are feeling out

of balance. Your MIMS, aka emotions, will tell you right away. Don't worry about short-term periods of being out of balance. As long as they are short-term, they are normal. If they are habitual or persistent, you have one or more mind immobilizers running in the background. Resolve the inner conflict as quickly as you can and realize that it is detrimental to your system's performance. Don't get discouraged if this step doesn't happen all at once. You didn't build those habits overnight. And remember, it's much more fun not being stressed by the mind immobilizers. Choose fun!

2. Perform a regular MIMS check-up. Your mind is busy learning all the time and it is possible for you to pick another habit that is not beneficial while you are trying to rid yourself of your current mind immobilizers. Regular maintenance will ensure that new mind immobilizing habits are caught when they are still easily manageable. Old ones that we didn't catch before may also emerge.

3. Upgrade and maintain your mind environment. A better system allows better performance and more possibilities. To do so, you need to take action in improving your mind's strength. Start with little things. Change small habits like closing the door or brushing your teeth by using your other hand. Increase the level of difficulty gradually by changing different routines, from smaller to bigger ones. Give your brain more challenging tasks: learning something new, solving problems or puzzles that require effort. Replace the mindless activities with doing something deliberate that requires mental effort. You are working your brain "muscles" and preparing it to take you to new heights. Mind strength is a big factor in the creation of your desire. Meditate.

4. Work on your physical condition. Your body hosts your mind. The better your body feels, the better your focus is. If you are fighting a cold, how easy it is to be involved in an activity that requires concentration? Pay attention to your diet. Try to exercise regularly. Take care of your body in any way that is good for it.

5. Understand what your emotional filter is. Zoom in on the things that make you happy or the things that make you appreciate their beauty or perfection. Focus on them and don't shy away from spending time in admiration. It could be anything: from the perfection of nature and wildlife to beautiful and inspiring moments with other people. Enjoy the beautiful screen in front of you as much as you can. Go for gratitude.

6. Express yourself. Don't be afraid to be who you are. There is a powerful being inside that is longing to unleash its potential. Express yourself in the way you dress, the way you laugh, the way you dance, the way you talk, the way you work on your projects. When you are in the zone, stay there as much as you can and go back for more when you can.

7. Recharge yourself regularly. Meditate, spend time in nature, exercise, go to massages or do anything that makes you feel recharged so that your prefrontal cortex can work hard for you to succeed.

8. Be selective about what you point your attention to. Don't just focus on whatever's in front of your eyes. Deliberately and consciously choose the objects of your attention. Realize that some things are beneficial, while others are not.

9. Spend time appreciating who you are. You are a wonderful and unique combination of characteristics that makes you who you are. Focus on all the great things about you. Smile at yourself. You are perfect, reaching for more perfection every day.

10. Listen to your own voice. It knows what's best for you. Don't let others choose the path for you. You are in the driver's seat. You are in charge of your destiny. You have a voice. And it is powerful.

12. Set the background music of your life. Make it the way you enjoy it in every moment: upbeat, happy, inspiring, powerful, heavy, thought provoking, relaxing, mysterious, playful. You are the one that

can choose the tone of your life. Your life will dance to the rhythm that you've set.

13. Look for things that bring you joy. Find ways to enjoy everything that you do.

14. Strive toward success. Focus on the things that work well in your surroundings. Spend time noticing them and thinking about them. Be selective about what you watch and what you read. Establish a pattern of success by observing success. Give yourself credit for the little victories. Focus on your little victories and pat yourself on the back. If you fail, realize that failure is an important part of the success. Pat yourself on the back for having gone through the failure with courage and learn from it. Pat yourself on the back for not giving up. Surround yourself with people who have been successful in any area.

15. Focus on the present, because that's where your power lies.

16. Remember that you don't need to follow up on any of your desires. When time comes for action, you will be called and you will hear the call.

17. Make sure to turn the world around you off and turn your visualization on. Visualize the emotionally resolved you in situations that feel familiar, but have the crucial element that your desire has been realized in them. How would you feel and act if you had what you wanted?

18. Clean your closet.

Here are the eighteen steps charted out as if you were a computer. I've used the computer analogy, so that every time you sit in front of your laptop or look at your phone, your actions will begin to trigger these eighteen steps, solely by your normal everyday actions. This way, you've already gotten a head start on assimilating to this successful way of life. The steps go:

FULL SYSTEM CLEANUP - locate and reduce the mind immobilizing habits.

REGULAR VIRUS SCAN - watch for new mind immobilizing habits.

PROCESSOR, MEMORY, HARD DRIVE - train your brain "muscle."

MOTHER BOARD - take good care of your body.

MONITOR - change the way you see things. Appreciate.

KEYBOARD - express yourself. Don't be afraid to be who you are.

POWER SUPPLY - recharge yourself regularly.

MOUSE - be selective about what you point your attention to.

WEBCAM - love yourself. You are worthy of it.

MICROPHONE - you have a voice. It's powerful. Listen to it.

SPEAKERS - set the tone in your life. Life will respond to the rhythm you've selected.

JOYSTICK - look for things that bring you joy.

OPERATING SYSTEM "SUCCESS" - observe success in everything and give yourself credit for big and small wins.

"NOW" CLOCK - your power is in the present moment.

ON/OF SWTICH - turn the outside world off and start creating the future. Visualize.

REMINDER - clean your closet (Just kidding).

The best way to create what you want is to create a good mental environment. Before you can climb a peak, you have to have a good "mind muscle." Years ago, I would regularly get together with friends after work, where I would drink and party until late at night. Mornings would always be difficult and after a while, I was tired all the time. A friend invited me to go on a hike once. It sounded like a great idea, but once we got on the trail, I realized that I was far from prepared for it. It was a very challenging trail, making me wish I could order a cab right there to take me back home.

Not long after, my constant tiredness pushed me to make a change. I started going to the gym, jogging every morning, and soon my body was toned and strong. Still, I never forgot the difficult trail, so I decided to go give it a try again. When I started hiking, I thought for sure I had mixed up the difficult trail I wanted to re-try with a beginner's trail. It was too easy! But I hadn't missed it. It was the same trail. Only I was different. I was stronger and what once seemed like an impossible endeavor was now an easy journey.

When you are climbing a peak, if you have muscles that are not ready, the journey is hard and often impossible. Sometimes you have to get off the trail, get your muscles stronger and return when you are ready.

Do your mind preparation, so you can be ready for your peaks. Find the emotionally resolved you. Don't wait until tomorrow. Start now. You have a whole life of desires to manifest.

Now go have some fun! Start looking for things that make you happy. Reach for your emotionally resolved self. Go play. There is absolutely nothing wrong with you or your life. You haven't messed up. You are standing on a platform of potential. You are seeded for success. Go get happy, so you can realize your potential. You are perfect. The best part of your life is yet to unfold. It's not about facing life. It's about creating life. Happiness is the key. So go ahead! Start using that magic wand! You are ready to fulfill your dreams.

Acknowledgements

I want to thank my parents for their unconditional faith in me. I also want to thank my brother who taught me that you don't need to have perfect life in order to be happy and have fun. Big thanks to Dr. Courtland Ofelt who opened my eyes to beauty, gave me a platform for growth and supported me in everything I dreamed of achieving. Big thanks to my dearest Marzena Hartford - if we didn't look so different, I would have suspected that she is my long lost twin sister. She encouraged me and supported me in ways that nobody else can - she always finds the perfect approach. I want to thank Vicki Lis: She guided me into spirituality, opening the doors to a wealth of knowledge and love. She gave me nothing but unconditional love, teaching me by her example. I owe a great deal of my growth to her. I want to thank Jeff Peterman for teaching me self-love and how to celebrate life. He helped me to release my deepest fears and allowed me to see life from a more liberated perspective. I am very grateful to my wonderful cat who taught me unconditional love. Thanks to Steve Jones, who inspired me to start writing. Lots of gratitude for Esther Hicks for her incredible teachings. And finally, big thanks to my wonderful and patient editor Casey Greenberg.

References

1.McLeod, S. (2007). Pavlov's Dogs | Simply Psychology. Retrieved July 30, 2015.

2. Arnsten, A. (2009, June 10). Stress signalling pathways that impair prefrontal cortex structure and function. Retrieved July 31, 2015.

3. Arnsten, A. (2009, June 10). Stress signalling pathways that impair prefrontal cortex structure and function. Retrieved July 31, 2015.

4. Barkley-Leveson, A., & Crabb, J. (n.d.). Bridging Animal and Human Models. Retrieved July 31, 2015.

5. Chabris, C., & Simons, D. (2010). The invisible gorilla: And other ways our intuitions deceive us. New York: Crown.

6. Wright, A. (n.d.). Limbic System: Amygdala (Section 4, Chapter 6) Neuroscience Online: An Electronic Textbook for the Neurosciences | Department of Neurobiology and Anatomy - The University of Texas Medical School at Houston. Retrieved July 31, 2015.

7. Stress Effects on the Body. (n.d.). Retrieved July 31, 2015.

8. List of Emotions - Human Emotional Chart. (2008). Retrieved July 31, 2015.

9. BUCKNER, R. (n.d.). The Brain's Default Network Anatomy, Function, and Relevance to Disease. Retrieved July 31, 2015.

10. Carroll, L. (1984). Advice from a Caterpillar. In Alice's Adventures in Wonderland & Through the Looking-Glass. New York, New York: Bantam Dell.

11. Moran, T. (2005, June 1). Kuznets's Inverted U-Curve Hypothesis: The Rise, Demise, and Continued. Retrieved July 31, 2015.

12. Argh, J. (2012, May 11). Priming Effects Replicate Just Fine, Thanks. Retrieved July 31, 2015.

13. Boeree, C. (n.d.). The Limbic System. Retrieved July 31, 2015.

14. Pine, K. (n.d.). Karen Pine, Psychologist, Author & Speaker. Retrieved July 31, 2015.

15. Adams, C. (n.d.). PROMOTING SELF–COMPASSIONATE ATTITUDES TOWARD EATING AMONG RESTRICTIVE AND GUILTY EATERS. Retrieved July 31, 2015.

16. World Meteorological Organization World Weather / Climate Extremes Archive. Retrieved July 31, 2015

17. Lepper, M., & Greene, D. (n.d.). Undermining Children's Intrinsic Interest with Extrinsic Reward. Retrieved July 31, 2015.

18. Lally, P., C. H. M. van Jaarsveld, H. W. W. Potts, & J. Wardle. How are habits formed: Modelling habit formation in the real world. Eur. J. Soc Psychol., (2010). V 40. Retrieved July 31, 2015.

19. Winerman, L. (2011). Supressing the 'white bears.' Retrieved July 31, 2015.

20. Grohol, J. (n.d.). 15 Common Cognitive Distortions. Retrieved July 31, 2015.

21. Moseley M.D., B. (2002, July 11). A Controlled Trial of Arthroscopic Surgery for Osteoarthritis of the Knee — NEJM. Retrieved July 31, 2015.

22. Cheever, S. (2004). My name is Bill: Bill Wilson : His life and the creation of Alcoholics Anonymous. New York: Simon & Schuster.

23. Rock, D. (2009). Your brain at work: Strategies for overcoming distraction, regaining focus, and working smarter all day long (1st edition ed., p. 279). New York: HarperCollins.

24. Confirmation Bias. (n.d.). Retrieved July 31, 2015.

25. There's a Name for That: The Baader-Meinhof Phenomenon. (2013). Retrieved July 31, 2015.

26. Winerman, L. (2005). The mind's mirror. Retrieved July 31, 2015.

27. Giant Sequoia tree. (n.d.). Retrieved July 31, 2015.

www.ingramcontent.com/pod-product-compliance
Lightning Source LLC
LaVergne TN
LVHW011326080426
835513LV00006B/221